AM I DOING THIS RIGHT?

HOW TO LIVE OUT YOUR FAITH THROUGH
THE WISDOM FOUND IN JAMES

Written by Erica Wiggenhorn
Designed by Morgan Broom
Copyright © 2024 by Proverbs 31 Ministries
All Scripture quotations are English Standard Version (ESV) unless otherwise noted.

WE MUST EXCHANGE WHISPERS WITH GOD BEFORE SHOUTS WITH THE WORLD.

Lysa TerKeurst

PAIR YOUR STUDY GUIDE WITH THE FIRST 5 MOBILE APP!

This study guide is designed to accompany your study of Scripture in the First 5 mobile app. You can use it as a standalone study or as an accompanying guide to the daily content within First 5. First 5 is a free mobile app developed by Proverbs 31 Ministries to transform your daily time with God.

Go to the app store on your smartphone, download the First 5 app, and create a free account!

WWW.FIRST5.ORG

WELCOME
to JAMES

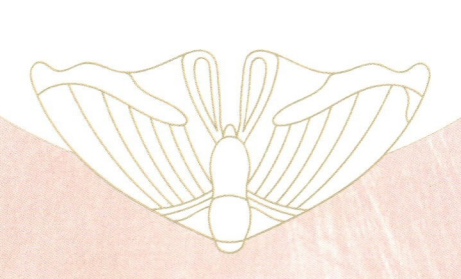

As I listened to her words, I found myself rubbing the cross necklace hanging from my neck. I simultaneously gazed at the canvas bracelet around my wrist and read the words "What Would Jesus Do?" With emotions swirling and my gut tightening, all I kept thinking was, *What is the right way to answer?*

I had no idea if I should simply apologize to this person or try to defend myself or if my own frustration over the conversation was even justified. Should I turn the other cheek or set a firm boundary? I wished Jesus would miraculously show up and hand me a script of what He would want me to say.

How often do we face situations in life where we can't quite pinpoint the "right way" to respond?

Difficult family dynamics, financial stresses, parenting choices, church conflicts, relational decisions ... so many areas where we wish we had immediate access to all of God's wisdom to apply to our specific situation.

That's where James comes in with his refreshingly practical five-chapter handbook of principles for wise Christian living. Exactly half of his letter consists of commands dealing with "every area of a Christian's life: what he is, what he does, what he says, what he feels and what he has."[1]

James' primary concern for his readers was the issue of practically and wholeheartedly living out their Christian faith. Attitudes, practices and priorities of the world had begun to infiltrate their lives, pulling them away from a life guided by Jesus. Their thoughts became fractured by worldly philosophies and ideals, causing confusion over how they should navigate the various cultural issues they faced. James' readers seemed to be listening to competing worldly voices offering advice on how to respond to the troubles of their time. And today we, too, have endless opportunities to find the world's "wisdom" for our varying situations.

Thankfully, James reminds us of God's wisdom through the ages, referencing over 21 Old Testament books as well as many teachings of Jesus, and offers sure guidance for our day. By pointing us repeatedly to the faithfulness and generosity of our God, who promises to give us all we need to follow His will for our lives, James also brings tender encouragement. He invites us to experience true gospel community where the love of Jesus guides our actions and fuels our faith. In the process of arriving at *what to do* as Christians, we discover *how to be,* transforming our relationships and our own perspective.

Jesus is coming back for His people to take us to a whole new reality — the heaven He has prepared for us. Earthly things that loom large in our daily lives diminish in contrast to God's power over them and His care for us.

When we don't know what to say ... when we wonder what to do ... James says to turn to God's Word. Through Scripture, the Lord will provide wisdom, perspective and power. And as a part of God's Word, the book of James brings us not just theoretical ideas about God but day-to-day resources for godly living.

Got questions? Help is here. Let's go get the answers we are seeking together.

What joy to journey alongside you,

Erica

WHO WAS JAMES?
A Lost Brother Found

Imagine spending your life antagonistic toward someone, maybe even fighting against them or demeaning them, only to discover later that you had the person all wrong. From what we can gather based on Scripture, this was James' experience with Jesus.

James was Jesus' brother (a son of Mary and Joseph) and grew up in the same household as Jesus: They would have eaten meals together, run around their father's workbench, and most likely slept in the same room. No one else saw the day-to-day Jesus over the course of many years in quite the way James did. Yet it seems James initially did not believe Jesus' claims to be the Son of God, nor did he promote His ministry. Scripture says *"not even his brothers believed in him"* (John 7:5).

The Gospels also do not record James attending Jesus' crucifixion. But after Jesus' resurrection, He appeared to James directly after He appeared to His 12 chosen apostles and a crowd of over 500 other disciples (1 Corinthians 15:6-7). Why James? Scholars suggest Jesus had additional siblings, but for a reason we are not told, Jesus singled out this brother, choosing to appear to him in His resurrected state.

During Jesus' earthly ministry, James, along with the rest of Jesus' family, once sought Him out while He was preaching and healing in northern Israel. Due to the large crowd, they could not get near Him, but someone approached Jesus, informing Him of His family's desire to see Him. Instead of stopping His preaching, Jesus replied, *"My mother and my brothers are those who hear the word of God and do it"* (Luke 8:21, emphasis added). Jesus' claim that His spiritual family was even more important than his earthly family was very countercultural in ancient Israel and would have been shocking. This incident undoubtedly left an impression upon James. Interestingly, he would later use very similar phraseology in his letter: *"But be doers of the word, and not hearers only, deceiving yourselves"* (James 1:22, emphases added). According to some scholars, James references the teachings of Jesus more than any other New Testament author.

After Jesus' post-resurrection appearance to James, which apparently led him to faith in Jesus as the Messiah, he rose to a position of prominence in the early Church. Many scholars date the writing of the book of James (originally a letter to the early Church) around A.D. 40, about a decade after Christ's crucifixion and resurrection.

If this date is accurate, it would mean James' letter was also one of the earliest writings of what we now know as the New Testament.

James served as the head of the church in Jerusalem, where Christianity was still widely considered a sect of Judaism. Christians therefore remained protected under Roman law to worship their own God apart from the Roman pantheon. But the Jewish religious leaders sought to separate themselves from Jewish Christians, feeling that Christians preached a false Messiah. So they stirred up trouble for their Jewish brothers and sisters who chose to follow Jesus and to believe in His resurrection and messianic claims.

Throughout his time as a church leader, James directly challenged the Jewish aristocracy and even priests of his day who were Jewish by birth and claimed to revere the Law of the Torah (the Old Testament) yet treated their brothers and sisters in oppressive ways. His bold outcry against them undoubtedly sparked their fury. While James remained opposed to taking violent action against injustice, he fearlessly faced threats of violence against the Church with bold rhetoric and reminders of God's judgment for those who spited God's commands.

According to the ancient historian Josephus, James was ultimately martyred in A.D. 62 by the high priest in Jerusalem for his unwillingness to renounce Christ.[1] Known for his piety and benevolence to the poor, he became nicknamed James the Just. The people in Jerusalem respected him so much that Jewish religious leaders worked for the removal of the high priest after James' execution, even though they themselves were not followers of Jesus.

WHAT ISSUES DID JAMES & THE EARLY CHURCH FACE?

As the head of the Jerusalem church, James was called upon as an authority on how to navigate two topics in particular: Jewish Christian worship requirements and gentile inclusion into Christ's Kingdom.

Jerusalem remained the center of Jewish religious life due to the location of the temple. But not long after Jesus' crucifixion, great persecution broke out against the followers of Jesus there (Acts 8:1). The religious rulers in Jerusalem imprisoned Jesus' apostles once, forbidding them to speak about Him. Then some religious leaders instigated false witnesses to accuse Stephen, an early Church leader, of blasphemy, for which they stoned him to death (Acts 7). One Pharisee in particular, Saul, oversaw the execution. This catalyzed the flight (or diaspora) of many Christians from Jerusalem to the surrounding areas. For this reason, James' letter is addressed to *"the twelve tribes in the Dispersion"* (James 1:1).

Around A.D. 34, Jesus appeared to Saul, the same Pharisee who had persecuted early Christians, and commanded him to stop persecuting His people and to take the message of Jesus to the gentiles (Acts 9). Saul, who also went by the Greek version of his name, Paul (Acts 13:9), became an apostle and missionary like James, sent out directly by Jesus Himself (Galatians 1:1; Galatians 1:12-17).

Paul began to preach the gospel of grace throughout the regions of Cilicia and Syria. But it appears some took his message of grace and twisted it, leading others to believe obedience to God was no longer necessary because their sins had been forgiven in Christ. Correcting this misunderstanding of Paul's message became a predominant theme in James' letter. Grace spurs us on toward greater obedience out of gratitude, not an attitude that says, "Live however you like since you're going to heaven anyway."

As Paul's ministry spread, greater numbers of gentiles began to convert to Christianity. A debate broke out: Do these converts need to follow all of the laws of Judaism or not? A real hot button was the ritual of circumcision (Genesis 17). To answer this question, James headed up the Jerusalem Council, along with Paul, Barnabas, and a gathering of apostles and elders. Peter weighed in with his thoughts. Paul and Barnabas relayed their miraculous conversion stories, and James delivered a ruling. We clearly see the authority of James here along with his handling of the scriptures — specifically, Amos 9:11-12, which he quoted in an eloquent fashion (Acts 15:1-21).

James did not rule out the necessity of obedience and lifestyle change for a follower of Jesus, but he did assert that strict adherence to Judaism was not required.

James did not say gentiles must stop sinning *in order* to be saved. Rather, he communicated that once a person becomes saved by faith in Jesus, they willingly submit to obeying God as a response to the salvation they've received. Scholars debate the exact meaning of James' directives to *"abstain from the things polluted by idols ... and from what has been strangled, and from blood"* (Acts 15:20), but we do know these practices were widespread in the worship of Roman gods. Gentiles often worshipped multiple gods simultaneously, so James' directives centered around the fact that following Jesus means worshipping Him alone. Here we see James' immensely practical side, which will also shine through in his letter, and his plea for wholeness in a believer's life. Following Jesus means committing to Him wholly, forsaking worldly forms of worship.

During James' ministry, there was also economic unrest in Israel: "Many peasants worked as tenants on larger, feudal estates; others became landless day laborers in the marketplaces."[1] With many barely able to survive, economic tension ran high. Some landowners even had their own squads of hired assassins who would be sent to deal with uncooperative tenants. In the area surrounding Jerusalem, religious zealots known as the "sicarii" would secretly murder Jewish aristocrats who exploited the poor.[2] Various outbreaks of violence occurred frequently. This highly marginalized society with very few exceedingly wealthy people and masses of struggling poor people constituted James' primary audience. His practical advice for dealing with political and economic tensions may categorize his letter as "the most relevant New Testament book for the 21st Century, especially the Western Church."[3]

THE MOST IMPORTANT PERSPECTIVE:

Hope for Our Questions

James promised a day of divine reckoning for the unjust, which he knew could happen very soon. This time of judgment will occur upon the return of Christ, and He Himself says no one knows when that time will be except the Father (Matthew 24:36). Instead of reading James' promise of judgment as *immediate*, we can understand it as *imminent*. Now that Jesus has already come, died on the cross and risen again, He will return for us. And when He does, He will gather His people to be with Him forever, He will judge the world, and He will bring to account those who have refused to believe in Him.

From James' vantage point and ours, this could happen at any time. So we live in assurance of that promise. Any injustice we face here on earth will be avenged by the authority of Christ. This promise cautions us not to seek our own vengeance against people who sin against us and comforts us when we struggle to keep the faith. Our God cares about our difficulty. We are not abandoned or forgotten. He is not indifferent to our pain.

And as we await Jesus' return, James' direct and practical teaching allows us to navigate complex theological truths and arrive at easily adoptable applications. How do we follow Jesus in varying circumstances? James walks us through a biblical how-to process to arrive at workable conclusions. James originally wrote his letter to believers who had been removed from the familiar and influenced by their surrounding culture. He addressed those who were crying out for justice and taught them not to incite violence with their actions or stir hatred with their speech. He opposed wordly ways of thinking and implored believers to care for one another in practical ways along with remaining committed to prayer. In a world where we live with constant streams of information telling us how to think, live and believe, James' cut-to-the-chase commands help us weave our way through the noise and live out our faith moment by moment.

JAMES' TRUTH FOR TODAY:

The Wisdom We Need Is in the Word

James' letter, filled with a myriad of Old Testament references, also quotes Christ Himself and uses vivid word pictures that bring his points to life, all providing strong calls to action in a believer's life. James uses the images of forest fires, horses, ships, moth-eaten clothing and rusting metal to paint pictures of the principles he teaches.

The tone of his letter is pastoral. No fewer than 15 times, he refers to his readers as *"brothers"* or even *"my beloved brothers,"* meaning fellow members of God's family of faith.[1] His purpose is not so much to inform us of a particular theology or doctrine but to provide applicable encouragement for our daily lives. The result is a string of imperatives or exhortations, with the overall message that we are to remain steadfast in following Jesus, keep cultural influences from weakening our faith, and pursue a community of love and care for others, especially our fellow believers.

One term unique to James is "double-minded." He refers to the double-minded man twice in his short letter (James 1:8; James 4:8), depicting someone who is easily swayed, lacking wisdom, strength or resolve. The answer to this double-mindedness, James says, is to cleanse our hands and purify our hearts (James 4:8). These cleansing rituals represent a process of preparation in order to properly worship God.

In other words, James advises us to intentionally pursue Christ in all things. We don't sway back and forth between the ways of the world and the way of Jesus. We commit ourselves fully to Christ to become *"perfect and complete, lacking in nothing"* (James 1:4). James does not teach that sinlessness is possible on this side of heaven, but we strive for holiness and obedience as we seek Christ with all of our being.

In James' day, Jewish believers in Christ began to experience something they never could have imagined: They worshipped the risen Messiah, Jesus, alongside gentile believers! For their entire existence, Jews had been taught to remain set apart from gentiles. Now they intermingled socially and culturally with gentiles and had to discern which lifestyle choices honored Christ and which ran contrary to His teaching. James addressed this conflagration of opinions as people became exposed to new ideas. The pinnacle or crescendo of his letter came in James 4:4, where he sharply rebuked, *"You adulterous people! Do you not know that friendship with the world is enmity with God?"*

How do we live in the world but not be like the world? James makes it clear in his letter: We wholly live for Christ, allowing Him to make us whole in the process. So let's buckle up for a ride of straightforward truth and practical encouragement in the book of James!

MAJOR MOMENTS

WEEK 1

James 1:1-4
James encouraged perseverance in trials for spiritual maturity.

James 1:5-8
James encouraged asking God for wisdom without doubt.

James 1:9-11
Worldly riches are temporary.

James 1:12-15
Giving in to the temptation to sin leads to spiritual death.

James 1:16-18
All good gifts come from God.

WEEK 2

James 1:19-21
James emphasized listening and humbly accepting God's Word.

James 1:22-25
God calls us to obey His Word, not just hear it.

James 1:26-27
True religion means caring for the vulnerable and being unstained by the world.

James 2:1-4
James warned against showing favoritism based on social status.

James 2:5-7
God has chosen the poor to be rich in faith.

WEEK 3

James 2:8-11
Christians are called to keep the law of love.

James 2:12-13
James instructed Christians to live mercifully as those judged by the law of liberty.

James 2:14-17
Faith without deeds is dead.

James 2:18-20
James taught that even demons believe in God, but they don't live for Him.

James 2:21-24
No one will be declared righteous without righteous works.

WEEK 4

James 2:25-26
James reminded his readers that Scripture is full of examples of imperfect people who acted in faith.

James 3:1-2
James pointed out that church leaders and teachers will be held responsible and should control their words.

James 3:3-5
The tongue is a small thing that has dangerous power.

James 3:6-8
The tongue can be like a fire that no one can tame.

James 3:9-12
It is unnatural and inconsistent to bless God while cursing others.

WEEK 5

James 3:13-16
Envy, selfish ambition and earthly desires lead to disorder and evil.

James 3:17-19
True wisdom from God is pure, peace-loving, considerate, full of mercy, impartial and sincere.

James 4:1-3
Quarrels are caused by selfish desires.

James 4:4-6
God opposes the proud, and friendship with the world is enmity with God.

James 4:7-10
James told his readers to submit to God, resist the devil, and humble themselves before the Lord.

WEEK 6

James 4:11-12
Slandering and being excessively critical violate God's law.

James 4:13-15
Boasting about tomorrow is not showing proper humility.

James 4:16-17
If we know the good we ought to do and do not do it, it is sin.

James 5:1-3
James warned against hoarding wealth and exploiting others.

James 5:4-6
James assured that rich oppressors will face judgment.

WEEK 7

James 5:7-9
James taught that Christians can be patient like a farmer waiting for rain.

James 5:10-12
James encouraged Christians to consider the prophets and Job as examples to have integrity in our speech.

James 5:13-15
James urged believers to pray for those who were in trouble, were sick or had sinned.

James 5:16-18
The prayers of the righteous are powerful.

James 5:19-20
Bringing a wandering believer back to faith is a noble act.

week one

AM I DOING THIS RIGHT? HOW TO LIVE OUT YOUR *Faith* THROUGH THE *Wisdom* FOUND IN JAMES

FAITH

wisdom

AM I DOING THIS RIGHT?
BOOK of JAMES | *Faith Through Wisdom*

JAMES 1:1-4

DAY 1

James encouraged perseverance in trials for spiritual maturity.

In the opening of his letter, James jumps right in and splashes us with the cool, refreshing water of God's promises for how to live out our faith, specifically in times of suffering.

When we navigate difficult days, we often crave definitive direction. We want to know what to say and do to make our circumstances better. But often, in complex situations, life doesn't provide simple answers. We want to employ the quickest means possible to improve the situation. Who wants to drag out difficulty?

But even in the not-knowing, we can take comfort in the assurance that God is accomplishing something in us and beyond us, bringing purpose to our pain. James starts with the beautiful promise that when life feels challenging, Jesus is changing us in ways we cannot always see in the moment. God often accomplishes His most epic work through chaotic circumstances. Our difficulties are not design-less. God always has a purpose to perfect us (James 1:4). James explained that trials may feel bad, but God works through them to conform us to His image and help us grow in *"steadfastness"* (James 1:3).

- What is a challenging circumstance you are currently facing?

- How could God be using this circumstance to make you more like Jesus? (It may be tempting to gloss over this or arrive at a quick answer, but try to really sit with this question for a minute or two.)

We may know that God's goal is to make us more like Jesus, and we may even desire this, but what does it actually mean? Oftentimes we think of this in a guilt-focused way. We should be kinder. We should be more patient or more loving. We think of developing Christlikeness as though it's a spiritual chore. But how is it *beneficial* to be more like Jesus?

Let's think about that for a minute.

Jesus always knew the right thing to do.
Jesus always knew the right thing to say.
Jesus knew when to step away and replenish Himself.
Jesus knew how to set healthy boundaries.
Jesus did not worry about what other people thought of Him.
Jesus resolutely trusted God.
Jesus endured *"trials of various kinds"* (James 1:2), including a literal trial before a *"council [that was] seeking false testimony against Jesus that they might put him to death"* (Matthew 26:59), yet He remained committed to the Father's plan.

When life feels confusing, difficult, disappointing or unfair, Christ in us allows us to respond with His wisdom. Through His power, we can view our circumstances from a much broader perspective and respond more purposefully than with mere human emotions.

- How could being more like Jesus enable you to *"count it all joy"* (James 1:2) in your current circumstances?

- What did Jesus say about trials in John 16:33?

James says trials can make us steadfast. That's a spiritual way of staying "stable" or "constant." God's constant, steadfast love for us is mentioned throughout Scripture — including over 125 times in the book of Psalms alone.

- What does Psalm 31:7 say about His love?

When we go through unstable and shifting circumstances, our steadfast God carries us and changes us. James implores us to be joyful in trials because they can make us more like Christ: stable, constant and strong.

JAMES 1:5-8 | DAY 2
James encouraged asking God for wisdom without doubt.

Sometimes reading the Bible can feel confusing. The word pictures may not always feel relatable. Most of us probably don't have millstones in our yards — or oxen yokes either. James will give us lots of word pictures in his letter, and sometimes we may wonder how they fit together, but in today's reading, his analogy of ocean waves is one of the most familiar to us.

- What did James compare to ocean waves in James 1:6?

Especially when life gets hard, we may tend to believe our doubts and doubt our beliefs. Satan wants to use doubt to weaken our faith; we see that he has been coming at humanity with doubt from the beginning, when he slithered up to Eve and hissed, *"Did God actually say ...?"* (Genesis 3:1). James, however, says to doubt our doubts and believe our beliefs. James 1:8 uses the word *"double-minded"* to describe one who lets doubts lead her astray or throw her around in confusion. If we let doubt creep in, we'll be like a wave tossed about: unstable.

But God longs to provide order and stability for our lives, and when we ask Him for wisdom, He will graciously give it — not begrudgingly or sparingly but abundantly (James 1:5). We just need to ask for it, then commit to following through on what God tells us to do.

These truths James teaches are a continuation of the first four verses of his letter, systematically linking the ideas together. Faithful believing leads to faithful behavior and spiritual blessings beyond that. These are not isolated bits of wisdom but truths bound together as a whole, bringing wholeness to our lives. Yesterday, we heard James remind us that trials in this life prove inevitable, but we can be joyful *in* them because of the work God does *through* them. Therefore, James instructs us to ask God for wisdom for our hard circumstances (v. 5). These commands work together.

- Why do we especially need wisdom when it comes to trials and difficulties?

- The book of Proverbs contains general wisdom for life, and James echoes a lot of the same language. What benefits of seeking wisdom from God do we find in Proverbs 3:7-8 and Proverbs 3:21-24? What do these mean to you? Meditate on these and describe them here:

The original readers of James' letter faced great difficulty. Many Jewish Christians had been uprooted from their lifelong homes and communities and relocated to new areas because of their faith in Jesus.[1] Imagine the questions they faced: Where should they go? Would there be difficulties in their new location? Should they attend the local synagogue in their new area? How would they support themselves financially? James brought these wrestling believers great encouragement in his command to ask God for wisdom. He promised that God would give wisdom generously and not fault them for asking.

- Why might these early believers have been hesitant to ask God for wisdom in their situation? In what circumstances do you hesitate to talk to God, and how does James 1:5 encourage you?

God's wisdom is not just a nice treat, a cool bonus or a take-it-or-leave-it suggestion — it is the perfect answer to every question we have.

Psalm 18:30 says, *"This God—his way is perfect; the word of the Lord proves true; he is a shield for all those who take refuge in him."* God's answer is not always an easy answer, but it is always the right answer that will lead to our righteousness.

- In what areas of your life do you need wisdom from God today? In what areas have you already received wisdom and you just need to take the next step to obey it? Write out your intentions here:

JAMES 1:9-11

DAY 3
Worldly riches are temporary.

James presents two groups of people in two separate positions in today's passage: the *"lowly"* in *"exaltation"* and the *"rich"* in *"humiliation"* (James 1:9-10). The concept of lowliness suggests someone who holds little significance according to the world's standards. This person often goes unnoticed and unrecognized. The world says their contribution does not count. Yet as believers, we who are lowly in the world have become exalted in Christ. Instead of basing our value on the world's standards, James invites us to see ourselves as God sees us: chosen, loved, redeemed and cherished.

- What attributes, titles or positions does our world value today? How does our culture treat people differently based upon these worldly values?

Counterculturally, James said the rich man could only boast in *"humiliation, because like a flower of the grass he will pass away"* with his wealth (James 1:10). Scholars debate which rich people James might have been referencing, whether fellow Christians or nonbelievers. Regardless, James' point remains clear: Our value as people does not reside in worldly wealth or powerful positions. Those things are neither eternal nor secure — unlike God's promise to *"[raise] us up with him and sea[t] us with him in the heavenly places"* (Ephesians 2:6).

This is a promise we can depend on, much like displaced believers in James' day had to depend on God to help them start a new life.[1] At the time, Jesus was regarded as a political insurrectionist by the Romans and a false Messiah by the unbelieving Jews, and following Him brought humiliating persecution that caused many Christians to flee from their homes. They were cast out of their communities. Many would have found themselves scrambling to find new means of livelihood in areas of the Roman empire that had cultural standards and religious ideas that were new to them.

- In what area of your life do you sense an especially deep need to depend on God?

- In Matthew 6:24, Jesus says we will serve Him or be devoted to something else. As an example, what other master does He mention specifically?

- What does Psalm 49:16-17 teach us about the brevity of life and worldly possessions?

Scholars tie today's verses together with James' opening verses on trials (James 1:2-4). The displacement of Jewish Christians from Jerusalem, which created economic disparities, was not the only trial the Church faced at the time, but it certainly was a pressing one.[2] In light of this struggle, James clarified that the rich should not think more highly of themselves than others. They could not count on their money to solve all their problems or heal their hearts. In fact, the poor, not the rich, could *"boast"* of a spiritual advantage (James 1:9) since they were learning of God's faithfulness to provide for their physical needs.

Today, our culture entices us to believe worldly success solves the problems of our souls — but the endless ache for more stuff proves nothing on earth can fill our void. We could own everything the world sells and still feel empty. Jesus alone fills that cavern of craving within us. For love. For meaning. For purpose.

Whatever need you have today, friend, your God gives generously. Seek Him first.

JAMES
1:12-15

DAY 4

Giving in to the temptation to sin leads to spiritual death.

One strategy for studying the Bible is to pay attention to repeated words, maybe even circling or highlighting them — they're usually important. So far in James' letter, we find three words he kept circling back to: *"trial," "test/testing"* and *"steadfast/steadfastness."* We see all three of these words repeated again in our reading today.

So far, James has spoken three truths to us regarding trials:

1. We will *"meet trials of various kinds,"* but God can use them to **strengthen** our faith (James 1:2-4).
2. God will graciously give us **wisdom** to see beyond the immediacy of our circumstances (James 1:5).
3. We should rely on God as our spiritual **provision** instead of earthly resources (James 1:11).

And in today's reading, James warns us that trials can open the door for temptation: We may be tempted to solve the problem ourselves by any means possible or scheme to end the trial as quickly as we can.

- Which of the above truths currently brings you the most comfort in your own difficult circumstances, and how might this help you resist temptation?

In our difficulties, we can be tempted to settle for a quick escape instead of seeking the *"crown of life"* (James 1:12), an expression James used to evoke the image of a runner winning a race and receiving a crown. In Roman culture, athleticism was highly valued and was a form of public entertainment. Winners of athletic competitions would receive a laurel wreath as a victor's crown. So, playing upon his call to endurance, James used the image of a crown to symbolize the eternal life that awaits all followers of Jesus after we run our race of faith.

- In what ways does your life right now feel like a long race demanding lots of energy?

- How does the promise of heaven and an eternity of no more trials give you hope to press on in faith despite your current circumstances?

When we grow weary and things feel too hard, our enemy slides up and hisses:
Is God really good, or is He holding out on you?
Can God really be trusted, or should you take this into your own hands?
Does God still love you, or is He disciplining you because He hates you?

Satan scatters seeds of doubt, hoping they take root in our souls. Yet James reminds us, *"Blessed is the man who remains steadfast"* and does not give up (James 1:12).

- Which seed of doubt do you need to dig up today and not allow to take root in your heart and mind?

In our trials, especially, we may be tempted to take action — even to do something we know is wrong — to seek relief or stop the pain. James 1:14 also uses the word picture of a baited fish hook ("lure") to describe this temptation. We see something we want and go after it. Often we don't think through the consequences. We don't see the hook because we're too mesmerized by the bait. But when we snatch at what Satan tosses at us, we choose sin, which leads to death (James 1:15).

- What are some practical ways to guard ourselves from temptation, especially when we feel weakened by difficult circumstances?

A GUIDED PRAYER FOR TIMES OF TEMPTATION

Dear Jesus, today I am struggling with

_____

Help me to remember that I never face any difficulty of which You are unaware and in which You are not working. I cannot understand what You are doing. It is hard to keep trusting. I know You have promised me heaven, where there will be no more trials, but today I also ask for Your strength to carry me through here on earth. I need Your wisdom to see how You are at work in my life. Guard me from the evil one, and keep me from temptation. I want to remain steadfast.

In Jesus' name, amen.

"Prayer is a *powerful* weapon in the hands of even the *humblest* believer; it does not require a super saint to wield it *effectively*."

DOUGLAS J. MOO,
THE LETTER OF JAMES

JAMES 1:16-18

DAY 5
All good gifts come from God.

You may have heard the saying, "If it seems too good to be true, it probably is." This generally refers to salespeople making promises they cannot keep. But this saying doesn't apply to God: He delivers on every single one of His promises. He will never fail us or forsake us.

James wanted his audience to remember this. He feared that some early Jewish Christians might be deceived and fall into sin. The Greek word translated *"deceived"* in James 1:16 is *planaó*, and it means "to wander or be led astray."[1] In this way, James indirectly referenced his Jewish Christian readers' current condition of displacement. Would they wander into their new pagan culture to the extent that they compromised their faith?

- What might be some examples of small and subtle moral compromises that the world considers "no big deal"? Why would Scripture call those same compromises *"deception"* (James 1:16)?

James reminded early believers in Jesus that what appears to be "good" still ought to be examined closely.

- For example, in Genesis 3:6, we find three potential "benefits" the serpent presented to Eve should she eat from the tree of the knowledge of good and evil. List those three benefits here:

God had already made it clear to Eve that she should not eat from the tree regardless of how alluring it looked (Genesis 2:16-17). While the fruit *looked* good to Eve, it was not good for her to eat because it required disobedience to God to enjoy it.

- What are some things you have said or done that seemed good at first but ultimately lead to consequences? How does today's reading in James encourage you to learn from these mistakes?

James says gifts from God are *"good and perfect"* (James 1:17, NLT). Then the metaphor switches from gifts to lights. Have you ever heard someone say, "That seems a bit shady"? Usually this happens when the person senses something hidden; the full truth is shadowed. That's exactly how Satan presents his "gifts." They *seem* good, but Satan holds back the whole truth.

- Have you ever received a gift that you sensed might have hidden motives behind it? How would this or did this make you feel?

James explained that God's gifts, however, are offered fully in the light. There's no fine print at the bottom of the contract, no hidden clauses to trick us, *"no variation or shadow"* (James 1:17).

And the greatest gift God gives us is our salvation. James moved to this point in verse 18.

- Whose *"will"* or desire brings forth salvation (v. 18), and how is this salvation accomplished? What do you think was the purpose of James mentioning this in connection with verse 17?

James said the early believers to whom he wrote his letter were the *"firstfruits"* of all who were to come (v. 18). In ancient agriculture, the firstfruits were the earliest crops from a field, indicating how bountiful the rest of the harvest would be. James invited his readers to view themselves as the beginning of God's great redemption of the world. The blessings that awaited them, and now await us, prove too numerous to imagine.

James implied both a promise and a command here in verses 16-18. Because his readers had received salvation and the Holy Spirit as firstfruits of the bounty that awaited them, they could rest in the promise that even greater blessings were coming beyond their earthly lives. In the meantime, he commanded them to stay steadfast in Christ and not to be deceived by sins that only *appear* good.

The same Jesus who saved us from our sins will see us through temptation and help us walk in His Truth. Our God keeps His promises.

"Whatever is good and perfect is a gift coming down to us from God our Father, who created all the lights in the heavens. He never changes or casts a shifting shadow."

JAMES 1:17, NLT

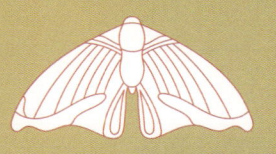

WEEK ONE

Reflection & Prayer:

Very few of us like trials. We'd rather stick with the tried and true and what seems good. If a store in your town handed out free samples of trials and tests, there probably wouldn't be too many takers. But life is full of trials. No person on this planet lives pain-free. We face financial crises, health scares, relationship hurts and losses of loved ones. We cannot escape the trials of this life.

James reminded us, however, that trials hold great purpose in our lives. God accomplishes something in our suffering that cannot be procured by any other means. We learn to rely on God's faithfulness, wisdom and resources, none of which are ever in short supply. As God orchestrates events around us, He is actively doing something in us — namely, making us more like Jesus. James defined this growth in us as *"steadfastness"* (James 1:3-4) rather than duplicity and instability. A sense of faith-filled confidence and wisdom develops in our lives as we rest in God's promises and surrender to His plans instead of striving and scheming in our own strength.

Dear Jesus, You know every hard thing we face today. There is nothing in our lives that goes unnoticed by You or is outside of Your concern. You care for us deeply and provide for us willingly. Give us wisdom to see how You are at work in our lives. Help us to understand how You are changing us from the inside out as we trust in You through our trials. We know You understand physical pain, loneliness, rejection, oppression, humiliation and death. Thank You that You never leave us alone in our trials and that through them, You are making us more like Yourself. In Jesus' name, amen.

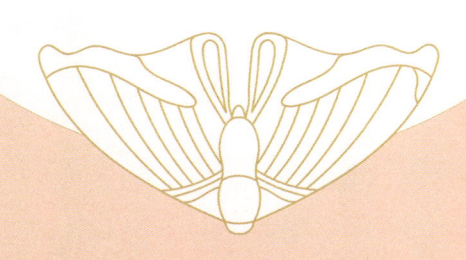

NOTES

NOTES

week two

AM I DOING THIS RIGHT? HOW TO LIVE OUT YOUR *Faith* THROUGH THE *Wisdom* FOUND IN JAMES

FAITH

wisdom

AM I DOING THIS RIGHT?
BOOK of JAMES | *Faith Through Wisdom*

JAMES 1:19-21

DAY 6
James emphasized listening and humbly accepting God's Word.

Have you ever been in a conversation with someone where it feels like they are not really listening to you? Instead, they are thinking about what their response is going to be before you have even finished talking. Or they blurt something out in the middle of your sentence.

- Describe someone who you consider to be a good listener: What do they do to let you know they are really trying to understand what you are saying?

- God gave us two ears but only one mouth — which may tell us something about how much we should listen compared to how much we talk. How might this apply to the teaching in James 1:19?

Most of the time when someone refuses to listen to us or says something that makes us angry, it provokes our pride. We feel slighted or treated unjustly. James' original readers had indeed been treated unfairly, both by the Romans and even by their own people since unbelieving Jews persecuted Christians. During this time in Israel's history, many zealots arose, encouraging others to react violently to oppression from governmental authorities. They certainly had cause to be angry. But dwelling in anger would not *"produce the righteousness of God"* (James 1:20).

- What circumstances make you angry because they feel so unfair? What are some passages of Scripture that help curb your feelings of anger and remind you to trust Jesus with the circumstances?

Sometimes even the Word of God will make us angry because it offends our pride. When 1 John 3:13 says, *"Do not be surprised, brothers, that the world hates you,"* our defenses go up. No one likes to be hated. Or when Jesus says, *"And if anyone would sue you and take your tunic, let him have your cloak as well"* (Matthew 5:40), we inwardly shout, *But that's not fair!* We long to justify why we do not want or need to obey these commands.

Yet just as James implored us to recognize God's Truth in the beginning of his letter, James 1:21 invites us to *"receive"* it. Instead of glossing over a Bible verse or going around it, trying to rationalize our current behavior so we don't have to change, James says to stop and really think about it. God's Word is *"implanted"* in us like a seed that grows if we embrace it *"with meekness"* (James 1:21).

- Do you currently have an area of your life where it feels hard or unfair to obey God? Describe the circumstances, and ask God for what you need to respond in humility instead of anger.

On our own, we are not humble and slow to anger. But God's Word *"is able to save [our] souls"* (v. 21). This crucial verse shows how James is aligned with the rest of the New Testament's understanding of salvation: Through God's grace bestowed by Christ's death on the cross — and through His Word, which God Himself plants in us — God saves us when we place our faith in Jesus. This will be important to keep in mind later when James emphasizes the necessity of doing good, which includes being slow to anger (v. 19).

Remember James 1:18? We are *"firstfruits of [God's] creatures."* We are a new creation, and God has *"brought us forth."* The NIV translation of verse 18 says He gave *"birth"* to us. This salvation changes our hearts, shifting us from a sinful bent toward evil and selfishness to a tendency toward goodness. It takes supernatural humility throughout this process to defy our calculated sense of what is right and fair and lay down what we think we deserve. But more than any effort on our part, it takes the work of God. Through the prophet Jeremiah, God promised, *"I will put my law within them, and I will write it on their hearts"* (Jeremiah 31:33).

- What else did God promise according to Ezekiel 36:26-27?

Those of us who are in Christ have God's Word written on our renewed hearts, empowered by the Holy Spirit enabling us to obey.

- How does it encourage you to know that God doesn't expect you to muster up enough strength to obey Him but instead He equips and empowers you to walk in greater obedience?

JAMES 1:22-25

DAY 7
God calls us to obey His Word, not just hear it.

We give different kinds of attention to things we encounter in the world depending on how valuable they are to us. If we walked by a diamondback snake, for instance, we'd probably stop and evaluate how to proceed without getting hurt. If we walked by a diamond gemstone, we'd most likely bend down and pick it up. We'd roll it around in our hands and examine it from various angles, deciphering its authenticity and worth.

James insists we should use this kind of wise discernment when approaching the Word of God: It deserves our full attention and directs our actions.

To experience the true *"liberty"* that comes from following God (v. 25), we cannot simply hear His Word or even know His Word; we have to apply it to our lives. James offered the analogy of stooping down and taking a really close look at God's law — and in fact, James says we can look *"into"* the law like a mirror that shows us who we really are (v. 25). As we absorb every detail of our reflection, we can then see any sin that needs to be removed from our lives.

- How does Hebrews 4:12 describe the Word of God? For those who may be very familiar with this verse, take a moment to slow down and see if you can make an observation about something you haven't noticed before.

- According to Deuteronomy 6:4-9, how often are we to think about God's Word? How could keeping God's Word in the forefront of our thoughts impact our attitude or behavior?

- Why do you think consistent, frequent reflection on God's Word is necessary for us to obey it as *"a doer who acts"* and not a *"hearer who forgets"* (James 1:25)?

The theme of humility that leads to obedience runs all the way through James 1. Our hearts are proud and continually have to be reminded of what God has done for us. The more we remember the terrible cost of our sin that Jesus paid for on the cross, the more we are inspired to obey Him in return.

Still, our flesh flinches when obedience feels hard. Following rules seems constricting. This is why it's important to remember that the *"perfect law"* mentioned in James 1:25 has become a *"law of liberty"* and not of oppression for those who trust in Jesus. Christ fulfilled the law for us, so now when we commit to obey God's law, we do so in freedom. Through careful examination of Scripture and willful application over time, our Savior's Spirit works within us, making us more like Jesus.

This may remind us of a parable Jesus told about two sons who received the same command from their father yet responded in two different ways.

- Read Matthew 21:28-31. Which son was the obedient one in the end? What warning does this give us about *hearing* God's Word versus *doing* God's Word?

Our actions reveal our hearts. Our feelings sometimes lag behind, but even when we don't "feel like" obeying, we can still choose to respond in faith that God's commands are for our good. James tells us we are blessed by the Word when we act upon it.

- What would it look like for you to act upon God's Word today in your home, workplace or school?

JAMES 1:26-27

DAY 8
True religion means caring for the vulnerable and being unstained by the world.

You may be familiar with the expression, "It's not what you say — it's how you say it!" Sometimes our words themselves may be kind, but they nevertheless convey a tone of annoyance or judgment. Other times we may speak difficult-to-hear words but with a tone of compassion and gentleness.

Imagine if we could hear James read his letter so we could really pick up on the tone of the words he shared in today's reading!

- How would you describe the tone of James 1:26-27? (Critical? Encouraging? Persuasive? Passionate? Can it be several of these things at once?)

God *spoke* the world into existence (Genesis 1). Words carry weight. James keeps reminding us of this fact as we continue on in his letter. Our words reflect what we believe. And if we believe we have been rescued, redeemed and delivered by Christ, our speech will be *"bridle[d]"* (James 1:26) to reflect that new life in us.

- A bridle is a device that gives the rider of a horse control over what the horse looks at and where the horse goes. Why do you think James used this metaphor to describe how we should control our words?

- What does Proverbs 18:21 tell us about the power of the tongue? What will happen to those who love it?

James juxtaposed words and actions at the conclusion of Chapter 1: He said care for the vulnerable reveals whether we are truly followers of God as we claim to be (James 1:27).

- How does caring for those who cannot give us anything in return reveal Jesus' love to the world?

- Read Acts 6:1-7. How was benevolence established in the early Church, and what were God's people *"full of"* that led them to benevolence (v. 3)?

Orphans and widows were among the least powerful and most disadvantaged people in the ancient world. There were no programs, shelters or governmental safeguards for these victims of tragedy. Instead, individuals cared for those in need.

In today's world, at Christmastime, we may see donation campaigns for organizations that help provide for women and children in need all around the world. These serve as annual reminders to care for those less fortunate — but as followers of Jesus, we are to live generously every day, not just once a year. And James 1:27 shows that generosity is relational, not just financial: *"Visit orphans and widows in their affliction ..."* (emphasis added).

Spending our time this way helps others and keeps us *"unstained from the world"* of endless wants (James 1:27). Jesus warned that our hearts will dwell where our treasure resides (Matthew 6:21). To share both our lives and our possessions with others helps us store up treasure in heaven, guarding our hearts against the worldly values of grabbing all we can on earth for our own enjoyment.

- According to 1 John 3:16-17, how do we practically reveal that God's love is alive in us?

The message of the world is greed. *"For all that is in the world—the desires of the flesh and the desires of the eyes and pride of life—is not from the Father but is from the world"* (1 John 2:16). Yet as Christ works in us, He also works through us, enriching the lives of those around us by our words and our deeds.

JAMES 2:1-4

DAY 9

James warned against showing favoritism based on social status.

Psychologists have coined terms for our human tendency to gravitate toward success and power ("Basking in Reflected Glory," or B.I.R.G.) and our aversion to defeat ("Cutting Off Reflected Failure," or C.O.R.F.). We long to associate with people who link us to importance — and not with people who don't. When we follow these longings, however, we become *"stained"* by the world, as James said in James 1:27. We begin to determine people's value based upon their accomplishments, appearance or possessions.

- In what areas of your own life do you tend to compare yourself with others, measure success or assign value based upon the world's standards?

Especially when we feel stuck or unable to accomplish what we want to get done, a good thing to remember is that we are human *beings* and not human *doings*.

- What is the value of each human life actually based on, according to Genesis 1:27?

Interestingly, James placed a teaching about partiality immediately after the command to care for orphans and widows. Instead of "cutting off" these marginalized members of society, James urges us to reach out to our fellow image bearers who are in need. He also prompts us not to view those who are wealthy or successful (*"wearing a gold ring and fine clothing"* [James 2:2]) as a means to gain success ourselves. Our motivation should not be to gain but rather to give.

- What did James' fellow apostle Paul say about giving in Acts 20:35, and what words of Jesus did he quote?

- Has someone ever been kind to you only to get something from you? How did that make you feel?

- To look at this from the other perspective, have you ever overlooked people with *"shabby clothing"* (James 2:2) and instead paid more attention to the best dressed? How can we avoid this?

The ground is level at the foot of the cross. Kneeling before Christ, we are all equal: desperate sinners saved by grace. We are all also handmade by God and infinitely loved (Ephesians 2:10; John 3:16) Does a good father love his daughter once she becomes capable of *doing* things for him or from the moment she comes into *being*? How much more it is with our Father God's love for us!

In the ancient world, people generally believed wealth signified God's favor: The righteous received tangible blessings, and worldly difficulty demonstrated God's displeasure. But Jesus refuted this idea, and James reminded his readers of this fact when he said, *"Show no partiality as you hold the faith in our Lord Jesus Christ"* (James 2:1).

- Read Jesus' words in Luke 6:24-26. Why do people in the conditions He listed need to be warned?

There is an old adage that says, "You never know God is all you need until He's all you've got." Those who have fine things may think they don't need God because they have everything the world has to offer — but the truth is we all need God. As believers in Jesus, we are to listen to and love one another regardless of earthly resources, especially in the *"assembly"* of the Church (James 2:2). The only reflected glory we bask in is the glory of Christ.

JAMES 2:5-7

DAY 10
God has chosen the poor to be rich in faith.

God's provision in seasons of desperation swells our faith. Honestly, though, it can feel safer to be inspired by other people's faith stories than to live in a chapter of desperation ourselves. For instance, we marvel at how the wandering Israelites in the Old Testament went to sleep every night trusting God to provide *"bread from heaven"* for them to eat the next day (Exodus 16:4) ... but in our own lives, it's hard to embrace a season of hunger that forces us to depend completely on God.

- What miraculous stories of God's provision have you heard of or personally experienced?

- Today's reading challenges us to consider a different perspective on earthly lack. In what ways is it better to be *"rich in faith"* than in worldly possessions, according to James 2:5?

- What warning about riches are we given in Proverbs 23:4-5? In contrast, what promise do we see in 1 Timothy 6:17 about God's provision?

In our world, the poor are often disregarded or mistreated. But God esteems the poor. This is evidenced, James argued, by the vast number of believers to whom God has revealed Himself through Christ but whom the world would consider poor (James 2:5).

That is not to say God disdains or disregards the rich: The early Church included rich as well as poor believers. But during James' lifetime, society in the Near East generally was made up of a small group of wealthy landowners and an educated class, with nearly everyone else being economically poor. The Apostle Paul pointed this out in his letter to the Corinthian church: *"For consider your calling, brothers: not many of you were wise according to worldly standards, not many were powerful, **not many were of noble birth**"* (1 Corinthians 1:26, emphasis added).

We must be careful not to say that Jesus' Kingdom is *only* offered to the poor. That would contradict scriptures that explicitly state that God is not partial (e.g., Deuteronomy 10:17). But God promises His Kingdom to *"those who love him"* (James 2:5), and many who love God are unloved or underprivileged in the world.

The key to wisdom about how to show proper respect to every person is to remember every person is created by *"our Lord Jesus Christ, the Lord of glory"* (James 2:1). Since all people are made in His image, and all believers are co-heirs of His inheritance, we are to honor them as such. In our churches, there are to be no pretenses. No comparisons of affluence. Just a gathering of believers celebrating grace. Everyone in the room openly admits being a sinner in desperate need of saving. When we look at our fellow brothers and sisters, we have the privilege of witnessing the presence of Christ Himself within them rather than rating outward appearances.

- In what ways can you resist the temptation to show favoritism to the rich or to dishonor the poor? How does Leviticus 19:15 explain a wise course of action?

WEEK TWO

Reflection & Prayer:

As believers, we can sometimes find pride creeping into our possessions, our positions and even our pews in the Church. The root of the behaviors James warned against in this week's readings is pride.

Humility is the opposite of pride, and James reminds us that humble people are teachable people. They look at others with an awareness that there is something to learn from everyone and that God created and loves each person, from the wealthiest to the least wealthy (James 2:5). In the realm of communication, humble people listen with love rather than only trying to prove their point (James 1:26).

James provided a word picture for us to explain how this looks in our everyday lives when he said *"put away all filthiness and rampant wickedness"* (James 1:21), using a garment analogy. We can pick up our sinful pride and put it away like dirty laundry. It doesn't belong on the floor — or anywhere — in the life of a Christ follower. Angry and selfish thinking will only trip us up. Instead, let's wrap ourselves up in the Word of Truth and obey it through God's power (James 1:22).

Lord, help us not to think less of ourselves but to think of ourselves less. Open our eyes to see the needs of those around us, and give us wisdom about how to help them. Reveal to us any areas of pride or partiality we have allowed into our thoughts and actions toward others. And keep our minds fixed on You above all! In Jesus' name, amen.

NOTES

NOTES

week three

AM I DOING THIS RIGHT? HOW TO LIVE OUT YOUR *Faith* THROUGH THE *Wisdom* FOUND IN JAMES

FAITH

wisdom

AM I DOING THIS RIGHT?
BOOK of JAMES | *Faith Through Wisdom*

JAMES 2:8-11

DAY 11
Christians are called to keep the law of love.

While James primarily forbids *"partiality"* in the context of wealth in today's reading (James 2:9), the Greek word he used here is plural, indicating the possibility of various forms of favoritism. This includes favoritism to the rich but could also include bias toward a particular ethnic group, people from a certain place, those with common interests, etc.

One seemingly benign way we imply favoritism toward the familiar is by saying about others, "I don't really have anything in common with them," which can mean we do not intend to pursue any sort of relationship with someone who is not like us. But followers of Jesus all share the common grace of salvation and the indwelling of His Holy Spirit, and that unites us more than anything else!

James brings strong conviction in today's passage, reminding us that partiality breaks God's law (James 2:9). That may sound a bit extreme, but since God's law is perfect, any imperfection in our obedience to it counts as sin, whether showing preference to people with certain educational levels, cultural backgrounds or achievements or doing something as extreme as committing murder (James 2:11).

- Often we think that if we do the right thing most of the time, we can consider ourselves to be good people. It's like if we got 9/10 questions correct on a test — we'd get a good grade, right? But how many laws can we break before we "fail" the "test" of God's law, according to James 2:10?

- Read Matthew 5:21-22 and Matthew 5:27-28. How do these scriptures relate to James 2:10-11?

The reality is that we all fail. No one has ever kept the whole law ... except for Jesus. And when we remind ourselves of the great sacrifice He made on our behalf so we do not have to face divine judgment under the law, we are overwhelmed by thankfulness and humility.

When James 2:8 refers to the *"royal law,"* we understand him to mean the Old Testament law, fulfilled in the words and actions of Jesus. For instance, we can look at Jesus' interaction with a prideful Pharisee named Simon in Luke 7:36-50. Simon invited Jesus over for dinner, wondering if Jesus might be a prophet. But when Jesus arrived, Simon did not offer Jesus a customary kiss of greeting, water to wash His feet, or oil to soothe His head. These simple acts of hospitality were commonplace in Israel, and Simon behaved rudely in his failure to offer them. Contrarily, a sinful woman who witnessed this humiliation of Jesus rushed to His feet, washing them with her tears and drying them with her hair. She poured oil upon Him, bestowing the honor Simon should have shown.

- Read Luke 7:40-50. What did Jesus imply as to the reason why Simon disregarded Him?

- Why would someone who thinks they don't need mercy have a harder time showing someone else mercy?

- How did Simon show partiality in this story, and how did Jesus show honor to the woman?

Simon was no less in need of forgiveness than the sinful woman. He just *thought* he was better than her. This self-righteous attitude had crept into the religious elite while Jesus was alive, and after Jesus' death and resurrection, James wanted early Christians to take this sin, and all sin, seriously.

We are all desperate sinners, but thanks be to God, He offers grace and forgiveness to all who call upon Him. In the same way, we are to offer grace to one another.

JAMES 2:12-13

DAY 12
James instructed Christians to live mercifully as those judged by the law of liberty.

We tend to judge ourselves by our intentions, but we judge others by their actions. In other words, we are generally more merciful to ourselves.

If a friend from church had surgery, for instance, and we verbally committed to arriving at her home with a meal but then didn't actually do so, she wouldn't judge based upon our good intentions. Her feelings would be hurt by our actions — or rather our inaction in following through with the promised dinner. But we might tell ourselves, *Well, I intended to do it ...*

- Have you ever had good intentions yet failed to follow through on your commitments? Who did it affect, and how did they respond?

James flipped this line of thinking on its head. He used present-tense, imperative verbs in James 2:12 when he said *"so speak and so act as those who are to be judged,"* meaning "keep on speaking and acting," holding us accountable for our actual behavior and not just our intentions to obey God. But he also gave us some good news: He claimed our judgment falls under the *"law of liberty,"* that is, the law fulfilled by Jesus (v. 12).

You may recall this is now the second time James has mentioned this *"law of liberty"* (James 1:25; James 2:12). It kind of sounds like an oxymoron, doesn't it? But it's true! Because we have been empowered by the Holy Spirit, we have now become free to fulfill not only our good intentions but God's intentions. We are no longer shackled by sin and selfishness. Instead, we can live the way Jesus lived.

- Does the idea of living like Jesus feel like a bunch of rules or like freedom to you? In what ways?

- How does James' encouragement that Jesus has empowered us to move away from habitual sin and selfishness bring you hope?

While Jesus' death on the cross paid for the sins of all who believe in Him, that does not make our obedience to Him unimportant. Empowered by His Spirit, we now follow His commands and treat others mercifully, the way He has treated us.

As such, we approach the plea for mercy in James 2:13 with an acknowledgment of our own sinfulness. Without Christ, if we were to ask God for justice, we would receive eternal death as the due punishment for our sin. But in Christ, we receive mercy instead of the judgment we deserve — because Jesus took our judgment on Himself.

- Read Luke 18:35-43. What request did the man who was blind make of Jesus twice?

- What do you think the crowd thought of this man's worthiness to receive mercy?

This man by the roadside was a sinner just like you and me. Jesus readily extended mercy to him anyway and healed him.

Our extension of Christlike mercy to those the world may view as unworthy speaks volumes about our faith. Mercy flowing through us proves Christ's presence in us. We cannot keep the whole law, no matter how pure our intentions, but we can draw on the strength and righteousness of Christ. And when we long to do good but fail to follow through, we can cry out, *"Jesus, Son of David, have mercy on me!"* (Luke 18:38).

- Who can you show mercy to this week as a way of living out your faith in Jesus?

JAMES 2:14-17

DAY 13

Faith without deeds is dead.

Some of the most beautiful books are cookbooks. The ones with the colorful, glossy pages with the meal expertly arranged on a beautifully decorated table. But *looking* at a cookbook won't magically turn anyone into a culinary queen. The recipes provide more than enough information, and we may even have a drawer of kitchen tools, but until we do more with cookbooks than just look at them ... it's never going to happen.

That's the point of today's passage in James. If we say we follow Jesus, we are to do the things Jesus did. We have the teachings of Christ, the actions of Christ, and the empowerment of Christ through the Holy Spirit, so James says it's time to get to work! What good is it to have all of those things and just leave them sitting there unused? If we see a brother or sister in need and do not actually do anything about it, we fail to live out our faith (James 2:16).

- Why do you think it is important to Jesus that our inward faith in Him changes our lives (and others' lives) outwardly?

There are two important points to be made here. First, sometimes we will say as believers, "I wish I had more faith," implying that our actions would be bolder or better once our faith grew to a certain level. But James says we don't have to reach a certain "level" of faith before we see faith at work in our lives. Faith is meant to make a difference in us immediately as well as progressively through the lifelong process of the Holy Spirit making us more like Christ.

- How does James 2:14-17 echo Jesus' words in Luke 17:6?

Second, James is not saying we are saved by good works, but he does say that faith leads to good works. Saving faith in Jesus makes a difference in our lives. It sets us free to extend mercy to others. Just like cookbooks don't really do any good unless we do something with the knowledge within them, faith isn't truly faith unless we put it into action.

- In what area of your life do you find yourself wishing you had more faith? How does James inspire you to put your faith into action?

- In Matthew 25:31-46, how does Jesus describe those who are saved by faith?

In other words, what good are good wishes? We cannot spread pious lip service of "peace" to someone who is hungry and naked, ignoring their physical needs while preaching the gospel of a God who wants to meet their needs.

James spoke specifically of believers caring for *"a brother or sister,"* meaning fellow believers in Christ (James 2:15). That does not mean we have no responsibility to extend mercy to strangers or unbelievers, but James insists that unwillingness to help a fellow Christian, someone within our own faith family, especially brings the genuineness of our faith into question.

- How does Paul echo this idea in Galatians 6:10?

- What might be some practical ways we could increase our awareness of the needs within our churches and prayerfully consider how God may be calling us to help meet those needs?

BIBLICAL WORD STUDY:
Shalom

The Hebrew word for "peace" in the Old Testament is "shalom." According to the *Lexham Theological Wordbook,* "Peace denotes the wholeness, soundness, and well-being that characterizes God and that God created in the world. As peace was broken due to human sin, such well-being constitutes the hope for ultimate restoration by God."[1] A common ancient Hebrew greeting was "shalom shalom," meaning "perfect peace," a blessing in hopes that God's peace in a person's life would be made complete.

In Greek, the original language of the New Testament, the word for "peace" is *eirene* (where we get the English name "Irene"). The meaning of this word, especially as used by the writers of the New Testament, is more or less the same as that of "shalom." The idea is much broader than the absence of conflict; it includes peace in a political sense and in relationships both with God and with others in one's own life.

James used this word for "peace" exactly three times in his letter and one additional time as an adjective ("peaceable") rather than a noun.

James 2:15-16 says, *"If a brother or sister is poorly clothed and lacking in daily food, and one of you says to them, 'Go in **peace**, be warmed and filled,' without giving them the things needed for the body, what good is that?"* (emphasis added).

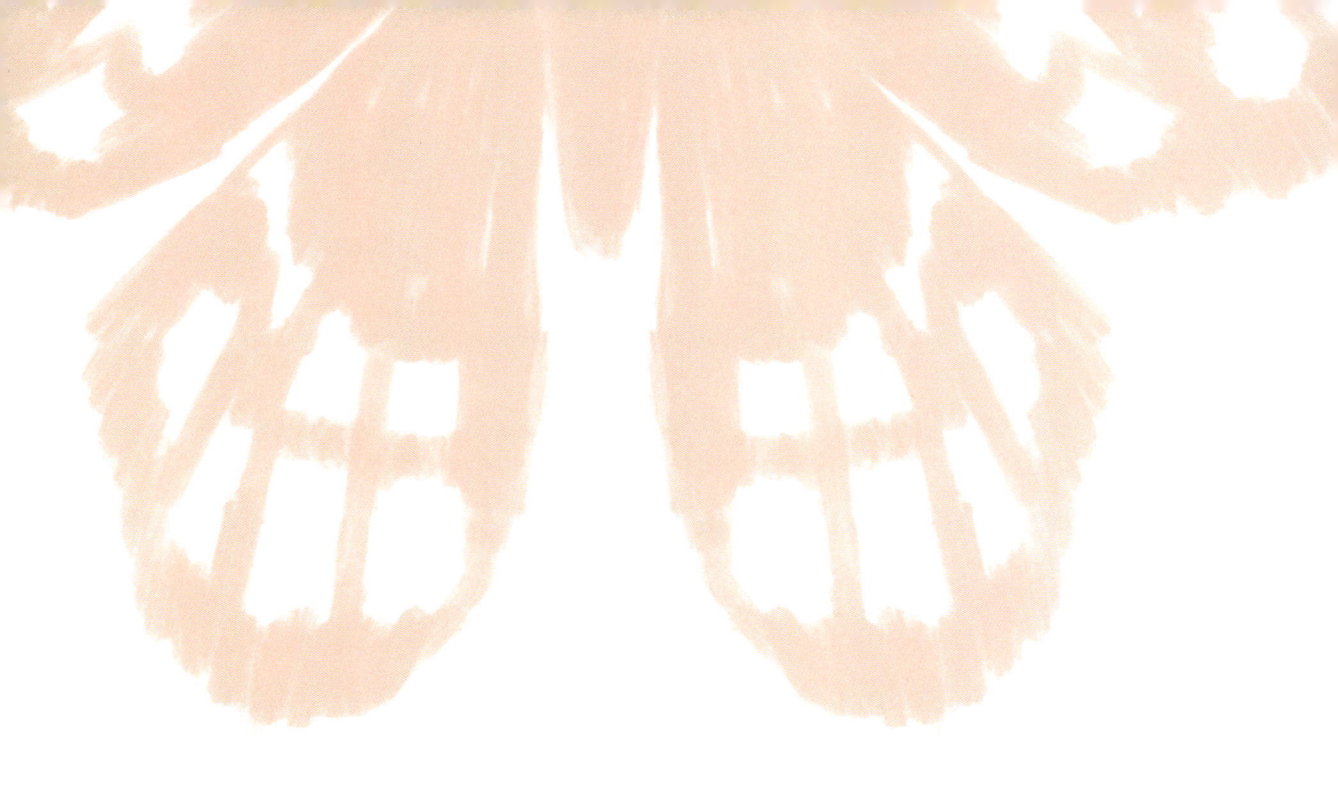

The shalom/*eirene* idea of wholeness and soundness is expressed in the inseparability of the physical and the spiritual. To care for a brother or sister in Christ includes bringing peace to the whole person, not merely meeting their physical needs to the exclusion of their spiritual or emotional needs (or vice versa).

James 3:17-18 says, *"But the wisdom from above is first pure, then **peaceable**, gentle, open to reason, full of mercy and good fruits, impartial and sincere. And a harvest of righteousness is sown in **peace** by those who make **peace**"* (emphases added). Here James highlights how godly peace results in interpersonal peace.

In the Old Testament, the presence of God's peace was a gift of His covenant with Israel but remained conditional upon Israel's obedience.[2] As New Testament believers, we receive God's peace due to the death and resurrection of Jesus Christ and the indwelling of His Holy Spirit within us (Ephesians 2:13-22). This pervasive peace is available to us at all times through the Holy Spirit. And to the fullest spiritual and practical extent, peace will be the result when creation is fully restored by Jesus upon His return at the end of the age.

JAMES 2:18-20

DAY 14
James taught that even demons believe in God, but they don't live for Him.

In big cities like New York, it's easy to find tents on the street where vendors sell "designer" handbags at bargain prices. Note the scare quotes — because while they appear to be designer handbags, these often are not genuine. The zipper may break and the straps crack within hours. The threads fray, and the quality doesn't hold up.

In today's section of Scripture, it could be argued that James says *"show me your faith apart from your works"* (James 2:18) in scare quotes as well, meaning someone may think he has faith without works, but in the end, it doesn't hold up. It is an imposter faith. James differentiates between appearance and substance. What might look like faith on the surface ultimately breaks, frays, cracks, and does not accomplish any practical change within us or around us.

James also differentiates between the faith of acceptance versus the faith of action. Suppose someone signs up for the army. They take the oath to join, walk up and sign the contract. They accept that there's a war to fight. However, the next day, when it's time to deploy and head to war, they are nowhere to be found. They took no action based upon their acceptance. When they needed to show up, they bowed out. Is that person really a soldier?

James insists that real faith works, or it's not really faith. *"Even the demons believe [in God]—and shudder!"* he says in James 2:19, but a true follower of God actually lives for Him.

- How did new Christians in Ephesus demonstrate the genuineness of their faith in Acts 19:18-20? What resulted from these believers giving up their former ways of life (see especially v. 20)?

- How do you see faith at work in your life?

Acts 8:9-24 is one story in Scripture that reveals how a person can believe in the person of Jesus but either not have faith in Him as Lord and Savior or else need to seriously grow in faith.

- Read Acts 8:9-13. Who was Simon, and how did he come to believe in Jesus?

- Read Acts 8:14-24. What happened when Simon saw the power of the Holy Spirit? What specifically did Peter implore him to repent of in verses 22-23?

Simon believed in Jesus, but he wanted to utilize His power for his own ends. He was motivated by greed and personal glory rather than God's glory. This is an example of James' point: Whether or not Simon had true faith is questionable, but it seems he sought gifts and not the Giver. He seemed to lack the true fruit of turning away from his sin. If that was the case with Simon, James would say, "That's not real faith!"

At this point, we might think, *Well, sometimes my belief in God doesn't match up with my actions ... Am I really saved?* Of course this is an important question — and ultimately only God can answer it. But we can note a few truths:

1. Every Christian still battles sin even after they are saved. On this side of heaven, no one lives out their faith perfectly — but that doesn't mean our salvation isn't real.

2. If we have placed our faith in Jesus, the Holy Spirit is continually sanctifying us, or changing us from the inside out. *"And we all ... are being transformed into the same image from one degree of glory to another. For this comes from the Lord who is the Spirit"* (2 Corinthians 3:18).

3. God says He will finish the good work He started within us when we put our faith in Jesus (Philippians 1:6). Anyone who has *"heard the word of truth, the gospel of your salvation, and believed in him, [is] sealed with the promised Holy Spirit, who is the guarantee of our inheritance"* (Ephesians 1:13-14). A guarantee from God is a sure promise.

When our faith holds up and shows up, the world will know we belong to Christ.

JAMES 2:21-24

DAY 15
No one will be declared righteous without righteous works.

You know that age-old question: What came first, the chicken or the egg? In today's scriptures, James answered a similar question about our faith: Which comes first, justification or good works?

James understood that as Christians, we are saved by grace through faith in the death and resurrection of Jesus Christ. We did not earn it, nor do we deserve it, but God offered us this salvation as a gift (Ephesians 2:8-9). Yet James also argues that our *"faith [is] active along with [our] works, and faith [is] completed by [our] works"* (James 2:22) just like Abraham's faith in the Old Testament.

- Read the story of Abraham offering his son Isaac to God in Genesis 22, particularly verse 12. Why do you think James referenced this story to show how faith and works go together?

It may appear that James 2:24 is saying we have to work to receive right standing before God. Theologians have debated this verse for centuries, but let's try as best we can to get to the heart of what it means. The idea of "knowing your audience" is crucial to our understanding. James was writing in response to the false definition of "faith" that we read about yesterday: a faith that is professed but does not produce any change in a believer's life. In reference to this, German theologian Dietrich Bonhoeffer coined the phrase "cheap grace," meaning that true faith costs us something: namely, laying down our own desires to accomplish Christ's desires, which is our lives' fullest joy and deepest meaning.

During James' lifetime, some Jewish Christians taught and believed that in order to receive salvation, people needed to follow the Jewish laws *and* believe in Jesus. Paul sharply refuted these "Judaizers," arguing that we do not live to follow a list of rules but to follow Christ (Galatians 3:19-21). At the opposite extreme, some other Christians decided that if we are saved solely by grace, then our obedience doesn't matter because God will forgive us (Romans 6:1-4). James balanced these two extremes: Although we are not justified by our works alone, our faith ought to influence what we choose to do. James would argue that no one really loves Christ without doing the works He calls us to do.

- If someone told you they loved you but had no desire to spend time with you or please you, would you believe them? Why or why not?

- What similar point did Jesus make in John 14:15?

James provides the example of Abraham to help us understand this to a greater extent. Abraham believed God *and* obeyed God. If Abraham had disobeyed God's request, it would have proven his lack of faith in God to fulfill His promise. But his willingness to offer Isaac demonstrated Abraham's faith (James 2:23). It became an outward manifestation of an inward reality.

- If we follow the example of the father in Mark 9:23-24, what can we do when we struggle to act on our faith?

- According to Romans 10:17, what else helps our faith to become increasingly active in our lives?

On average, there is only about 18 inches of space from our head to our heart. We spend most of our lives traversing that tiniest of distances. Does what we believe in our heads lead us to action based on the conviction of our hearts?

- What is an area of your life where you are struggling to act on the truth you believe about God? Cry out to Him today for grace to respond in obedience.

WEEK THREE

Reflection & Prayer:

Imagine packing a picnic basket, intending to take a bike ride to the park along the shore. Suddenly tornado sirens blast through your city. You know what the sirens mean, but you hop on your bike anyway, strapping the basket to the back and heading to the lake.

There really are only two possibilities in this scenario: Either you don't really believe the siren's warning of an impending tornado or you are not in your right mind. Because if you truly believed a tornado was headed your way, you would not choose to put yourself in the most dangerous place imaginable.

In the same way, James says if we truly believe Jesus is who He says He is, then we'll take action to avoid sin in our lives and we'll actively help others in our sin-shattered world. James held a theoretical debate in the middle of Chapter 2 with someone who foolishly tried to explain his faith without works. Maybe you have watched a television show or attended a conference where a moderator asked questions. In the middle of their answer, when they really want a point to sink in, the guest will turn away from the moderator and look directly into the eyes of the audience. James looks us squarely in the eyes in James 2:24 and declares, *"You see that a person is justified by works and not by faith alone."*

Our theological counterargument to James then becomes, "If I have to have works, how much work do I actually have to do to prove the genuineness of my faith?" But James' point is not that we should do good works to build a transactional record; rather, we focus on pursuing Christ. Is there a pattern of pursuing Christ in our lives overall? If not, going through this study is a great start!

Dear Jesus, sometimes I can get so bogged down by my behavior. I want to do better and be better, but I seem to find myself stuck in cycles of excuses or inaction. Help me to remember that You have given me the Holy Spirit, who continually works to renew me and help me grow in my faith. Thank You that You will never leave me and that You are always at work in my life. In Jesus' name, amen.

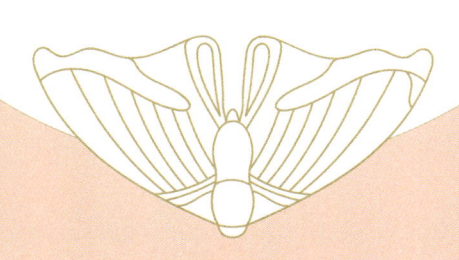

NOTES

NOTES

week four

AM I DOING THIS RIGHT? HOW TO LIVE OUT YOUR *Faith* THROUGH THE *Wisdom* FOUND IN JAMES

FAITH

wisdom

AM I DOING THIS RIGHT?
BOOK of JAMES | *Faith Through Wisdom*

JAMES 2:25-26

DAY 16
James reminded his readers that Scripture is full of examples of imperfect people who acted in faith.

Sometimes Scripture takes us by surprise. Let's pause and dial in on a phrase that might seem unexpected in today's reading: *"Rahab the prostitute [was] justified by works"* (James 2:25).

We meet Rahab in the Old Testament book of Joshua: When Israelite spies were sent to scout out the promised land, they stayed at Rahab's house in Jericho. She hid the spies because she believed God had given the city of her people over to Israel, and she asked to be spared when they conquered it (Joshua 2).

In James' day, many in the Church showed preference to the rich. They ignored the poor. So in an ironic twist, James pointed out a common pagan prostitute who became an example of righteousness. Rahab was a gentile woman who worked in a sinful trade. Yet here she is heralded as a hero.

- What does God view to assess a person, according to 1 Samuel 16:7? How does this relate to Rahab's story?

James' insistence that saving faith must be demonstrated by works may ignite our desire to quantify our obedience to God. We immediately want to know: *Well, how many good works or acts of charity do I have to demonstrate to be able to say I have true faith?*

James of course does not tell us. Instead, Rahab's example shows us that it is not perfect obedience that demonstrates faith but rather *a heart longing to grow in obedience.* In first-century Jerusalem, where James' original audience lived, a woman like Rahab would have been viewed with condescension and judgment, yet she serves as one of countless examples in Scripture of an imperfect person who put their faith into action. Having faith does not mean we will stop sinning altogether on this side of eternity — but it does mean we seek to please God with our lives, and the more we obey, the more our faith matures.

- Joshua 2 tells us of Rahab's first step of faith. According to Matthew 1:5-6 (an excerpt from Jesus' genealogy!), what became of Rahab?

- How does it make you feel to see that God honors our faith even though we are still sinners?

If Rahab had walked into the church James addressed in his letter, most likely she would have been ignored or even shooed away. Her background and social status would not have been welcomed. Yet James held her up as an example of a woman redeemed in the family line of Israel's beloved King David — and ultimately, King Jesus.

According to scholar Douglas Moo, the warning in James 2:26 is clear: "Without the spirit, the body ceases to be. In the same way, James suggests faith that is not accompanied by works ceases to be."[1] God grows and changes us through our faith in Him. That's what He did by transforming Rahab from a prostitute to a kingly progenitor — all by the work of grace. God's grace to Rahab, and to us, is unexplainable and beyond our comprehension.

- How does Rahab's story inspire hope that God is working within you, growing you and changing you?

- What do you hope your legacy of faith will inspire future generations to do and believe?

RAHAB
and the "Hall of Faith"

Rahab was not only heralded as a hero by James but also by the writer of Hebrews. In Hebrews 11, sometimes referred to as the "Hall of Faith," her name is listed alongside "giants" of our faith like Noah, Abraham, Isaac, Jacob and Moses.

"By faith Rahab the prostitute did not perish with those who were disobedient, because she had given a friendly welcome to the spies" (Hebrews 11:31).

In fact, besides Sarah, Abraham's wife (Hebrews 11:11), Rahab is the only woman mentioned by name in this litany of heroes. A gentile woman, once a prostitute by trade, nothing about Rahab shouted "heroic" by Jewish standards. But she became a hero to the Jewish people. Her story reminds us that God can redeem anyone by His grace, even the most unlikely people. He can reveal His wisdom to those who seem farthest from His ways. When we tend to jump to conclusions about others or feel counted out ourselves, let's remember Rahab.

JAMES 3:1-2

DAY 17

James pointed out that church leaders and teachers will be held responsible and should control their words.

In today's world, social media provides great power to the tongue. We have a platform from which we can propel our every thought into the universe. In some ways, this allows all of us to become "teachers" as we share our opinions, life experiences and viewpoints with the world.

- How do you see people on social media influencing our culture today?

In the early Church, there were teachers of the Bible — but not seminary-trained vocational ministers like we have today. Following the Jewish tradition, various church members could share a passage of Scripture and expound upon it. There was a select number of Jewish Christians who had studied under rabbis, such as Paul (Acts 22:3), but this was a small group. Still, a teacher held a position of honor, setting forth an example for others to follow. Before accepting this position, they needed to consider the responsibility of it.

- Why do you think we naturally hold people to a higher moral standard when they are vocal about their faith in front of large numbers of people? Is this an unfair or fair expectation of them?

No one can rightfully teach truths they aren't willing to live by. This was part of James' point when he said those *"who teach will be judged with greater strictness"* (James 3:1). James' teaching on taming the tongue applies to us all, but the weight of our words is especially heavy when we share them from a position of authority. This was one reason why Jesus spoke so negatively toward the Pharisees: They were the teachers of their day, but instead of pointing others to God, they pulled people away.

- Read Matthew 23:1-12. What sin do you see the Pharisees displaying in this passage?

- When Jesus says *"neither be called instructors, for you have one instructor, the Christ"* (Matthew 23:10), does that make it wrong to have Bible teachers? What do you think Jesus' point is here?

Jesus is the only perfect Teacher. He is the Word (John 1:1) and only speaks perfect words (John 6:68). All other spiritual teachers, along with every person on the planet, will stumble in what they say and fail to live up to what they teach (James 3:2). So one way to live out our faith is to respond with both grace and truth if we hear someone who claims to follow Jesus teaching something we believe to be unbiblical. First, we can trust that God knows and will hold them to account. Second, we can offer loving correction if appropriate, like we see in Acts 18:25-26 when two Christians encountered someone teaching an incomplete gospel: *"They took him aside and explained to him the way of God more accurately."*

- What did the people in Berea do in response to Paul's teaching in Acts 17:10-11? Why is it important for us to seek the Scriptures for ourselves, especially when we hear teachers sharing something that sounds new or unfamiliar?

God will hold all of us, and especially teachers, accountable for what we speak. So humility becomes the greatest guard for our mouths — the bridle that steers our body carefully (James 3:2). We also receive others' teaching with humility: If we sit under a teacher whose words rub us the wrong way, the Bereans provide an example of how to respond. We take our questions to the Word of God, trusting the Holy Spirit to guide each of us, teachers and listeners, *"into all the truth"* (John 16:13).

JAMES 3:3-5

DAY 18

The tongue is a small thing that has dangerous power.

Imagine hopping on a 1,500-pound horse and telling it where to go ... all with a 3-inch metal bit attached to reins. It doesn't seem possible that such a small piece of metal in a horse's mouth could direct it effectively.

We might think the same thing about our words: How important can they really be? They're just syllables and sounds. But in today's passage from James, we see that words direct our lives. This includes words spoken over us along with those we speak over ourselves and others.

In the ship example from James 3:4, we see how words chart our course in life. For instance, when we tell ourselves things like "I can't" or "it's too hard," we steer away from trying new things or maybe even from obeying God when He has called us to something. Likewise, if others have told us we are not smart enough, disciplined enough or capable enough, those words may drive us to forsake using our gifts for the Lord or to sabotage ourselves in other ways.

What we say informs what we do, and this often becomes our destiny. So James calls us to take all words to God, allowing Him to weigh their truth.

- Think of a time when you had hurtful words spoken over you. What did you do in response?

- Do you struggle with speaking hurtful words over yourself? Have you ever considered how those words direct your life's course? How have they affected your willingness to try hard things or step out in faith?

Friend, if you follow Jesus and the script that plays on loop in your mind is one of cruel self-condemnation, that is not a script written by Him (Romans 8:1). James 3:4 reminds us that we can change our words, and change our direction, according to *"the will of the pilot"* — and our Pilot is the God who speaks to us in love.

Colossians 2:14-15 (NLT) says, *"[Jesus] canceled the record of the charges against us and took it away by nailing it to the cross. In this way, he disarmed the spiritual rulers and authorities. He shamed them publicly by his victory over them on the cross."* Jesus has canceled and disarmed any condemning words spoken about you and over you once and for all, shaming them for shaming you.

- Whatever condemning inner script you most often find yourself rehearsing, write those negative words below, and then draw a giant cross over them.

Whether or not we struggle with self-shaming, many of us know firsthand how the tongue directs and drives and also how it can bring destruction. A single spark from a campfire can set a whole forest ablaze (James 3:5), and in the same way, one word can result in a conflagration of destruction. Words stir hearts and send people to action. In the most extreme cases, we might think of historical events like Hitler's rise to power in Germany. How could one person convince a nation to commit atrocities against humanity? It often starts with words. Many historians claim Hitler's charismatic speech stirred people to hate and hurt others.

In contrast, God's Word brings great healing.

- What does Psalm 107:19-21 teach us to do in our distress?

- According to Proverbs 12:18, how can our words bring healing to others?

One way we grow in wisdom is by meditating on God's Word, reading it, studying it, and recalling it in response to others' words. God speaks life with His words, and as His children, we seek to do the same.

JAMES 3:6-8 | DAY 19
The tongue can be like a fire that no one can tame.

In James 1:26, we learned from James that if we don't bridle our tongues, our religion is worthless. He then reminded us in James 2:12 to *"speak ... as those who are to be judged under the law."* In other words, we are to choose our words wisely. Next, the beginning of James 3 equated one's ability to bridle their tongue with their ability to bridle their whole body. We are not to forget how damaging our words can be and how easily we can utter words without considering their effect. The tongue has no bones but is strong enough to shatter a heart.

- In James 3:6, today we read that the tongue can set one's life on fire — but who or what sets the tongue itself on fire? What do you think this says about our hearts, minds and speech?

- Have you ever tamed a sea creature? Verse 7 says who has? With this in mind, what does verse 8 then say about the tongue?

In today's passage, James says the tongue *"stain[s] the whole body"* (James 3:6), which circles back to his previous teaching that true religion involves being *"unstained from the world"* (James 1:27). But if *"no human being can tame the tongue"* (James 3:8), what are we to do? Live our lives in silence?

Not necessarily. When James says our tongues are evil and poisonous in verse 8, he's using exaggeration to remind us to speak with extreme caution and discernment — but that doesn't mean we never speak.

- What are some practical ways you can use words to encourage, comfort, teach or serve others? What are practical ways to guard yourself against careless speech?

- What warning does Jesus provide in Luke 12:1-3 that sobers us to choose silence over speaking rash words?

Once words are spoken, they can only be forgiven, not forgotten. You may have heard from your parents as a child, "If you can't say something nice, then don't say anything at all," and silence truly is golden at times — especially in moments of anger. *"Even a fool who keeps silent is considered wise; when he closes his lips, he is deemed intelligent"* (Proverbs 17:28).

- When we are upset over something we wish we had not said, what should we do according to Psalm 120:1-2?

When we speak rash or harsh words *to someone,* we immediately see the effect of our words. When we speak *about someone,* we sometimes think their inability to hear our words renders them ineffectual. But if we talk about someone behind their back, we unfairly entice others to form opinions about that person based on our words instead of an actual relationship with the person.

- Has someone ever talked about you behind your back, leading others to form an untrue opinion of you? How did that make you feel, and what did you do about it?

In today's reading, James compares out-of-control speech to a raging fire (James 3:6). Perhaps another useful metaphor is that of a hunter, who would be foolish not to keep his rifles locked up tightly in a safe. Why? Because of how dangerous they could be if they got into the wrong hands. Scripture warns us that because our tongues hold life-and-death power, we are to guard them carefully.

God will help us guard our tongues when we ask for His help. He shows us when it is wisest to be quiet, and by His grace, we can speak words of life.

JAMES 3:9-12

DAY 20

It is unnatural and inconsistent to bless God while cursing others.

In his book *Christ-Centered Exposition: Exalting Jesus in James,* David Platt provides a poignant illustration explaining today's passage. Imagine an apple tree that produces nothing but rotten, mushy apples. The tree owner concocts a plan to cultivate juicy red apples from his tree. He goes to the store, buys a bag of ripe apples, and fastens them with a staple gun onto the branches. While sweet, crisp apples are now temporarily suspended from this tree, the apples produced by the tree remain rotten. The tree's problem resides in its roots. At its core, it is diseased.[1]

In the same way, we cannot simply "clean up our act" and work on better speech by our own power. We have a core problem: Within our hearts resides a sinfulness that must be addressed. Thanks be to God, the Holy Spirit is up to such a task when we willingly cooperate with His growth process.

- Have you ever tried to "clean up your act" as a Christian and be better in your own strength? How does it encourage you to know that the Holy Spirit longs to empower you with His power instead?

Our hearts are inherently selfish. We are inclined to burn with jealousy, take offense, grow bitter or lash out in anger. Jesus explains this sin problem in Mark 7:20-23: *"What comes out of a person is what defiles him. For from within, out of the heart of man, come evil thoughts, sexual immorality, theft, murder, adultery, coveting, wickedness, deceit, sensuality, envy, slander, pride, foolishness. All these evil things come from within, and they defile a person."*

- Of this list of heart battles, identify the one with which you are currently struggling the most. How can you admit to the Holy Spirit your need for His transformational power in your life and agree to cooperate with Him in this area? Record below what you sense the Lord speaking to your heart:

Praise God that the Holy Spirit has a better solution than a staple gun! He gives us new hearts (Ezekiel 36:26) and provides wisdom so we can see things from an eternal perspective. He always keeps His promises and finishes what He starts. As we submit ourselves to His transforming power, James 3:12 reminds us that we don't just add the good fruit of the Spirit to the old, rotten fruit of our flesh so that both are growing on the same tree. We become brand-new creations.

- According to Luke 6:43-45, if we consider ourselves to be like new trees that God has planted, how does Jesus show confidence in our ability to bear good fruit?

James 3 specifically says our new life in Christ includes putting a stop to the habit of criticizing and condemning other people, *"who are made in the likeness of God"* (v. 9).

- James' admonition certainly applies to our face-to-face conversations; how might we also apply it to communications such as social media, text messages or emails?

- How might imagining Jesus standing next to the person we are speaking with change our tone and/or words?

In the entire New Testament, we see the phrase *"Lord and Father"* only once: in James 3:9. These two names of God together insist that when we praise Him as our Lord — the highest form of speech we can utter — we also remember our relationship with Him as our Father. Contrarily, to curse our fellow people, whom God created, is one of the worst forms of speech we could utter. We can't say we love God but hate the people He has made. This echoes James' earlier warning about being *"double-minded ... unstable"* (James 1:8).

- Even for Christians, sharp or unkind words slip out of our mouths at times. Do you notice any patterns of when this happens in your life? Is it with a particular person, a certain time of day, or a certain circumstance, such as when you are tired, hungry or stressed?

- Think through conversations you've had recently, and ask the Holy Spirit to help you identify any unkind, impatient or hypocritical words. Write out James 3:10, and keep it accessible this week as you invite the Holy Spirit to continue to transform your speech into words of life. He is faithful!

WEEK FOUR

Reflection & Prayer:

This week's readings from James' letter could be summed up with the following statement: Our works and our words are either an expression of our faith or an expression of our fallenness. The tongue stains our testimony when our words contradict God, and the same goes for our actions when they contradict what we say we believe about Him. James says the tongue is *"set on fire by hell"* (James 3:6). Satan himself and our spiritual enemies, acting out of their fallen nature, give the tongue its destructive potential.

Yet as we wrap up this week focusing on the great power of the tongue to bring destruction, we can pause as followers of Jesus to witness how words are used for good by our God and Savior. As His children, we seek to emulate how He uses the power of words.

In the beginning, God used words to bring everything into existence from nothingness and to bring formlessness into order (Genesis 1). God also used His words to bless and provide direction to Adam and Eve: *"And God blessed them. And God said to them, 'Be fruitful and multiply and fill the earth and subdue it, and have dominion over the fish of the sea and over the birds of the heavens and over every living thing that moves on the earth'"* (Genesis 1:28).

Our words do not have the same power as God's, but what might it look like to use our tongues as instruments of peace in His name, bringing order and wholeness to the situations around us? How can we speak life into places devoid of hope?

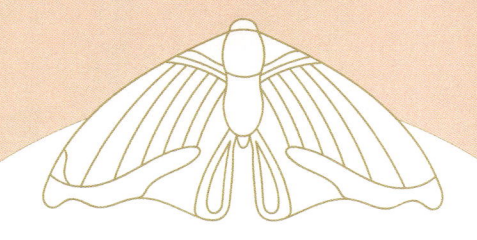

Dear Jesus, sometimes our world — and even our own internal dialogue — feels so noisy and filled with dissent, insults and arguments. Show us how to use our speech to bring life, peace and blessing to those around us. May those who interact with us feel refreshed by Your Spirit as we speak words of hope and kindness to them. In Jesus' name, amen.

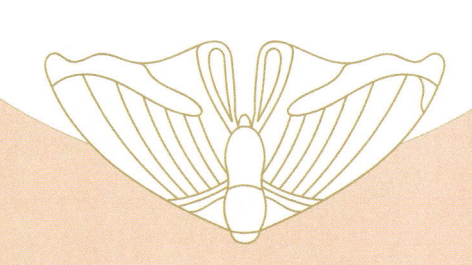

NOTES

NOTES

week five

AM I DOING THIS RIGHT? HOW TO LIVE OUT YOUR *Faith* THROUGH THE *Wisdom* FOUND IN JAMES

FAITH

wisdom

AM I DOING THIS RIGHT?
BOOK of JAMES — *Faith Through Wisdom*

JAMES 3:13-16

DAY 21

Envy, selfish ambition and earthly desires lead to disorder and evil.

The good life. That seems to be what our culture tempts us to chase at every turn. We often associate it with health, a "dream job," a house full of nice stuff, and happy kids. But James 3:13 says, *"Who is wise and understanding among you? Let them show it by their good life, by deeds done in the humility that comes from wisdom"* (NIV).

The world's pursuit of the good life focuses on pleasure and satisfaction now, in our flesh and in our pride. It is self-focused. James' definition of the good life focuses on wisdom and *"meekness"* (v. 13), or humility. It is God-focused.

- What connection do you see between humility and wisdom? Do you think it is possible to be wise without being humble, or humble without being wise? Why or why not?

- What works (outward words and deeds) display humility in a person's life? Contrarily, what works demonstrate the *"selfish ambition"* James references in verse 14?

Have you ever encountered a "one-upper"? If you share a funny situation, they have one even funnier. A difficulty? They have a disaster. A success? Their accomplishment surpasses yours. When someone longs to be the center of attention or cannot bear being outdone, they will boast over the extremity of their hardships or exaggerate their achievements. James packs a punch in verses 14-15 when he says boasting and self-promoting are *"demonic."* Yikes! When we engage in these behaviors, we are cooperating with evil beings.

To falsely boost ourselves up creates disorder (v. 16). In contrast, order reigns when we recognize that God is sovereign. We submit to His infinite wisdom and power in all areas of our lives, trusting His plans. He appoints, assigns and places people in the positions He has for them because He is all-wise.

- According to Daniel 2:20-22, how do people come into positions of power?

- According to Isaiah 46:8-11, who can thwart God's plans?

Disorder happens when we try to wrench God's plans from His hands, exalting our own wisdom above His. This is the very sin our enemy committed in the beginning. Satan was once an angel of God, but he wanted to be like God — all-wise and all-powerful (Ezekiel 28:14-19; Isaiah 14:13). And he tempts us to believe that God's wisdom cannot be trusted and that we must take matters into our own hands.

Let's close today by praying together:

Dear Jesus, forgive us when we rely on ourselves. We put our trust in our own plans and thoughts rather than in You. We long to make ourselves look better than we are so people will like us. We chase comfort and pleasure over Your purposes. Forgive us when we wrestle against Your will and Your way in our lives. Help us to be still and know that You are God. You have everything under control. Your ways are best. Where You have placed us holds great purpose. You know why we are there, and You will never leave us. Give us eyes to see what You long to do in and through us, and give us hearts willing to obey You. In Jesus' name, amen.

JAMES 3:17-19

DAY 22

True wisdom from God is pure, peace-loving, considerate, full of mercy, impartial and sincere.

Author Jerry Jenkins wrote a biography of Billy Graham, arguably one of the greatest evangelists of our day. He asked Reverend Graham what enabled him to preach so powerfully. Graham answered simply, "Search the Scriptures and pray without ceasing." This constant pursuit of direction from God guided Graham's life and filled him with wisdom to speak the Word of God boldly and with conviction.

James points out something tremendously important about wisdom in the two verses we will study together today: Wisdom comes *"from above"* (James 3:17), and God grants it to us as we seek Him. Two primary ways we gain wisdom are searching the Scriptures and spending time in prayer, *"ask[ing] God, who gives generously to all without reproach,"* as noted earlier in James 1:5-6. We can't manufacture wisdom or muster it up; we receive true wisdom from God alone by spending time in His Word and in His presence.

- Read Proverbs 2:1-8. How do these verses complement James' description of wisdom and its source?

Living according to godly wisdom is what James calls the *"good life,"* as we mentioned in yesterday's study (James 3:13, NIV). Jesus calls it the blessed life: Let's look at some parallels between the descriptions of godly wisdom in James 3 and the teachings of Jesus from His Sermon on the Mount.

- Draw lines to match each description of wisdom in James 3:17-18 to Jesus' teachings in Matthew 5:

James 3:17-18: *"But the wisdom from above is ..."*	Jesus' Sermon on the Mount
"Pure"	Matthew 5:5
"Peaceable"	Matthew 5:6
"Gentle"	Matthew 5:7
"Full of mercy"	Matthew 5:8
Full of *"good fruits ... and a harvest of righteousness"*	Matthew 5:9

Contrasted with the disorder and vile practices that come from worldly wisdom (James 3:16), wisdom from above results in peace and a harvest of righteousness.

Peace comes when we submit to God's authority. Even when we disagree with those in earthly authority over us, we respond peaceably insofar as they are not asking us to do something that compromises our biblical convictions. When people are peaceable, they are also productive. Rather than expending energy arguing, they pursue productivity in unison. If this is true in our workplaces, homes and communities, then it is doubly true in the Church, which, as we recall, was the original audience of James' letter.

A great harvest of righteousness also results when we choose to trust God's wisdom. The harvest imagery in James 3:18 would have resonated with Jewish Christians in their agrarian society: At the beginning of the season, farmers planted tiny seeds scattered across their fields, and at harvest time, bountiful stalks of wheat or countless baskets of *"good fruits"* (v. 17) would lead them to call their harvest "great." This is James' point: Small acts of mercy and gentleness will eventually grow into great acts of righteousness in our lives. We can start by extending grace to *"make peace"* (v. 18) with others, especially within the Church, not getting derailed into disputes.

- In which of your relationships do you most need the peace of God to yield a harvest of righteousness?

- How does focusing on the authority of God over this relationship allow you to let go of some control of it even as you seek to be *"gentle, open to reason"* and *"sincere"* (James 3:17)?

JAMES & JESUS:

Teachings on the Blessed Life

We mentioned early in this study that the book James often quotes or paraphrases Jesus' teachings (perhaps because James heard them so often, being Jesus' brother). Here are a few specific examples to compare and explore.

JESUS	JAMES	*How would you summarize these teachings?*
MATTHEW 25:34-40	JAMES 1:22; JAMES 2:15-17	
MATTHEW 5:3	JAMES 2:5	
MATTHEW 12:36-37	JAMES 2:12-13	
MATTHEW 15:11	JAMES 3:5-10	
MATTHEW 7:16-18	JAMES 3:11-12	
LUKE 18:14	JAMES 4:10	
MATTHEW 7:1-2	JAMES 4:12	
LUKE 12:16-21	JAMES 4:13-15	
MATTHEW 6:19-21	JAMES 5:1-3	
MATTHEW 24:33	JAMES 5:9	
MATTHEW 5:34-37	JAMES 5:12	

JAMES 4:1-3

DAY 23
Quarrels are caused by selfish desires.

Our social media feeds are often filled with inspirational and uplifting quotes ... but we probably won't come across too many excerpts from James 4 plastered across Instagram. The apostle was extremely direct here, apparently in response to extreme conflict among the believers to whom he was writing. A succinct paraphrase of his message could be: Unbridled desires within you result in drastic destruction around you.

Scholars disagree regarding how literally we ought to take the mention of *"quarrels"* and *"fights"* in James 4:1, but the Greek terms used here referred to military engagement, which suggests James does not want us to think of spats or minor disagreements only. Instead, he referred to intense clashes and combat: Envision soldiers on opposing sides, rushing toward one another, ready to fight. Some scholars assert that James 4:2a refers to actual murders in James' time, committed by zealots who justified their actions for religious reasons.[1] Others suggest James used this forceful language to emphasize his point, describing disagreements that had a warlike intensity if not actual wars.

Regardless, the starting point for application is clear: Our passions hold great power over us if we do not hand them over to the Holy Spirit for direction. The Greek word for *"passions"* in both verses 1 and 3 is *hedone,* from which we get the English word "hedonism" or "hedonistic," alluding to sensual pleasure.[2] This word is only used five times in the entire New Testament and negatively denotes pleasure and gratification.

- James 3:8 tells us that our tongues are *"full of deadly poison"* while James 4:2 tells us our desires can cause us to behave murderously. What connection does this make between our inner desires and our outward speech and behavior? What does this teach us about the condition of human hearts apart from Christ?

To *"covet,"* as mentioned in James 4:2, means to be jealous or envious of what someone else has. James also referred to jealousy in James 3:14 and James 3:16.

- Let's look at Exodus 20:17. What types of coveting are listed in the Ten Commandments?

- Describe some general reactions of people who *"cannot obtain"* (James 4:2) what they want. What is something you are longing for that you can lay before God today in surrender instead of coveting?

The solution to the immense conflicts within and around us involves prayer. James 4:2-3 suggests we are simply to ask God for the things we desire. God will not grant them to us if our motivations are wrong or if we merely seek earthly satisfaction at the expense of spiritual growth (though wrong motivations on our part are not the only reason God may say "no" to a prayer request). How beautiful to be invited to share the desires of our heart with a Father who loves us so much He will only give us what is best for us!

- Sometimes we might feel selfish or silly asking God for things that would bring us pleasure. What does God's role as our Father tell us about why He delights in His children coming to Him with our desires? How might bringing these desires before Him rather than sitting in jealousy shape our attitude?

- How does thanking God for the things we have curb our selfishness? What might it look like to pray *beyond* our own individual wants and desires?

When we ask God for something and we do not receive it, instead of becoming angry and jealous of those around us who have it, we can pause and reconsider. God only gives us what is best. A "no" today may become a "yes" tomorrow — but even if God never gives us that thing we've been asking Him for, we know He has a good reason. As the evangelist John Newton once said, "Everything is needful that He sends; nothing can be needful that He withholds."[3] And in cases where our desires are disordered and sinful, God's grace helps us to want His best for us instead. We can cling to the promise that *"it is God who works in you, both to will and to work for his good pleasure"* (Philippians 2:13).

JAMES 4:4-6

DAY 24

God opposes the proud, and friendship with the world is enmity with God.

Have you ever sat through a sermon as the message continued to build momentum to a point when the truth came crashing down on the congregation? Many commentators cite today's passage in James as an example of that climactic moment.

Did you pick up on a definite twist in James' tone here in James 4:4-6? The whole truth of his letter explodes in these few verses: As God's people, we will be tempted by many things the world will throw at us, but our allegiance must remain to God. The Church is the bride of Christ (Revelation 21:2), and placing our faith in anything or anyone else is like committing spiritual adultery — hence James' choice words in James 4:4a. Nine times up to this point in his letter, he had referred to his readers as his *"brothers."* Now he called them adulterers. Yikes!

Similarly, James said, *"Friendship with the world is enmity with God"* (v. 4b). In our culture today, "friendship" refers to something much different than it did in the ancient world. We have "friends" on social media we have never even met and know virtually nothing about. We refer to colleagues and acquaintances as "friends" even though we may know very little about their personal lives. But to the original readers of James' letter, friendship involved a close unity in which all aspects of life were shared.

- How would you define the concept of *"friendship with the world"* (v. 4) in your own words?

- God doesn't forbid us from being friendly toward unbelievers; Jesus Himself frequently ate with sinners, teaching and helping them (Mark 2:15-16). What do you think is the difference between Jesus' lifestyle and sinful *"friendship with the world"*?

James' next statement — that God *"yearns jealously over the spirit that he has made to dwell in us"* (James 4:5) — conveys God's desire to protect us from the evil within the world and keep our hearts close to Him. Scholars suggest this demonstrates God's holy jealousy for His people as His own rightful possession.

- How did Moses describe God in Exodus 34:14? How might this explain why God wants our full devotion (James 4:4)?

- In Galatians 5:19-21, what does Paul say will result from sinful human jealousy? How might this relate to our need for grace and humility as mentioned in James 4:6?

Verse 6 offers a beautiful promise: *"He gives more grace."* God will divinely empower us to remain faithful to Him while we war against our flesh. And this grace will likewise provide the power to subdue our fleshly desires. As the old hymn says, "O to grace how great a debtor daily I'm constrained to be. May Thy goodness like a fetter bind my wandering heart to Thee."

Being humble means admitting our desperation for God's grace to enable us to choose the better way — God's way — over the world's. James 4:6 is nearly a direct quotation of Proverbs 3:34, which says, *"Toward the scorners [God] is scornful, but to the humble he gives favor."* Humility comes from acknowledging that God holds a sovereign plan for our lives, and it is wise to submit to His plan because His ways are best. The world wants us to do things our own way, in our power and strength, but our God invites us to rest in His grace and care for us.

- In what area of your life do you most sense God imploring you to stay humble and faithful to Him? How does this promise that He will give grace in abundance help you?

We may feel as though we can never meet God's demands to love Him wholeheartedly. We may despair over our jealousy and envy of those around us. But God's grace will get us through. *"Now may the God of peace himself sanctify you completely, and may your whole spirit and soul and body be kept blameless at the coming of our Lord Jesus Christ. He who calls you is faithful; he will surely do it"* (1 Thessalonians 5:23-24).

JAMES 4:7-10

DAY 25
James told his readers to submit to God, resist the devil, and humble themselves before the Lord.

When the Spirit of God brings conviction, the people of God are driven to action. In the book of Acts, when the Holy Spirit powerfully spoke through Peter at Pentecost, calling people to repent, their response was, *"Brothers, what shall we do?"* (Acts 2:37). James' letter now pivots in this direction. When our hearts have turned away from God and toward the world, here is how to turn back to Him.

- Describe a time when you felt uneasy over some of your choices and inwardly sensed you were going against God's best for you. (That uneasy feeling, or "conviction," comes from the Holy Spirit sounding an alarm inside of us to warn us of sin.) Are there any sins in your life that you need to talk to Him about now?

In today's reading, James lays out an action plan for turning from our sin and living out our faith in God:

1. First, we submit to God (James 4:7a). This means we acknowledge God's wisdom is wiser than the ways of the world. We also recognize His rightful authority to direct our lives according to His wisdom.

Submitting is what we do. But practically speaking, *how* do we do it? This is what James addresses next:

2. We resist the devil (James 4:7b). The implication of the Greek word translated *"resist"* is "to stand against or to withstand." This infers a promise that whatever power Satan may have, we are able to overcome him by God's grace.

3. We draw near to God (James 4:8a). James appears to have had Hosea 12:6 in mind: *"So you, by the help of your God, return, hold fast to love and justice, and wait continually for your God."* Remember: James' commands and promises were written to believers in Jesus. But rather than love and justice, these believers had demonstrated selfish ambition and partiality. James was not necessarily talking about drawing near to God for salvation here, but he was referring to what repentance from sin looks like for Christ followers.

So when our hearts have wandered from God, how do we return to the close relationship with Him we once had?

4. We wash our hands and purify our hearts (James 4:8b). This alludes to how Israelite priests prepared to minister before the Lord in the Old Testament, reminding us that we are called to a high standard of behavior as Christ's people. He washes us clean through the gospel of His sacrificial death and resurrection, which we receive through the Word and which is how we draw near to Him (Ephesians 5:25b-27).

5. Finally we grieve, mourn and wail over our sin (James 4:9). When we draw near to God, we become saddened over our inability to fully follow the Lord's commands ... but our weeping turns to exaltation as we experience God's forgiveness of our sins through Christ (James 4:10).

All of these intentional choices result in our recognition of our deep spiritual need for our Savior. Thanks be to God that Jesus has rescued us and promises to present us, the Church, before God's throne as His beautiful bride!

- According to Jude 1:24, what is Christ able to do for us?

- On a scale of 1-10, how spiritually close do you feel to God today (10 being close, 1 being far)? Why?

- Of the five ways listed above to pursue closeness with God, which is easiest for you? Which is hardest?

Rather than trying to work our way into positions of power, recognition or status, we can humbly sit in the presence of God. He positions us for purpose and purifies our hearts. As we acknowledge our desperation for His deliverance, He will forgive and exalt us.

- Write out James 4:10 below, and also write down a circumstance or relationship in which you will commit to demonstrate humility.

WEEK FIVE

Reflection & Prayer:

G.K. Chesterton once wrote, "If I had only one sermon to preach, it would be a sermon against pride."[1] As we've mentioned throughout our study of James, pride seems to be the root of many of our problems. Jealousy and selfish ambition (James 3:14) are forms of pride. Jealousy says, "I am more worthy than you are to have what you have obtained." Selfish ambition says, "I am able to achieve more than others, and I deserve to keep what I have obtained for myself."

But Scripture encourages us toward humility, which is a byproduct of godly wisdom. Those who are aware of their own sinful nature; their physical, emotional and spiritual limitations; and their constant need to depend upon God's provision exhibit humility. They recognize that all they have is from God, whether their abilities, their accomplishments or their possessions. As Jesus clearly stated, *"I am the vine; you are the branches. Whoever abides in me and I in him, he it is that bears much fruit, for apart from me you can do nothing"* (John 15:5). Let's live out our faith every day with this truth in mind.

Dear Jesus, search my heart to see where pride exists in me. Give me wisdom to see where I am relying on my own strength or claiming accomplishments You have graciously allowed me to achieve by Your strength, power and wisdom. Guard me from the world's ways that tempt me to present myself as better than I am or to promote myself to gain positions or approval. May I remember Your warning that pride goes before disgrace, but those who walk with You in humility will be protected from pride's foolishness and exalted in due time. In Jesus' name, amen.

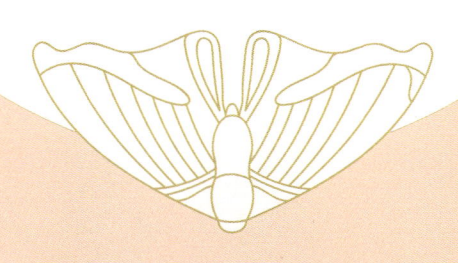

NOTES

NOTES

week six

AM I DOING THIS RIGHT? HOW TO LIVE OUT YOUR *Faith* THROUGH THE *Wisdom* FOUND IN JAMES

FAITH

wisdom

AM I DOING THIS RIGHT?
BOOK of JAMES | *Faith Through Wisdom*

JAMES 4:11–12

DAY 26
Slandering and being excessively critical violate God's law.

Last week, James firmly urged his readers to repent of their spiritual adultery (James 4:4) — but in today's reading, James shifted back to referring to his readers affectionately as *"brothers"* (James 4:11). His bold call to repentance completed, he now returned to exhorting them toward behavior that reflected obedience to God.

One way true repentance is demonstrated is by changed speech, as we see in James 4:11, which forbids *"speak[ing] evil"* and *"speak[ing] against a brother."* These are two translations of the same Greek verb, also meaning "defame" or "slander."[1] Ancient Jewish writings likewise called for repentance of the sins James mentioned in connection with speaking evil: jealousy, pride, selfish ambition, quarrels and double-mindedness.[2]

- How might jealousy, pride or selfish ambition lead to excessively critical or slanderous speech?

- How might excessively critical speech lead to quarrels and double-mindedness?

To *"speak evil"* (James 4:11) could include any of the following types of speech:

1. **Questioning legitimate authority.** A modern-day example could include criticizing your pastor to other people without speaking directly to the pastor himself.

2. **Speaking about others in secret in a way that feeds rumors or gossip.** For example, when friends spread gossip about someone based upon hearsay and with no productive reason for sharing the information.

3. **Bringing false accusations against someone.** According to Jewish law, which James' original readers knew well, slandering a person in court could lead to the false witness receiving the punishment the accused would receive under the law if found guilty.

- Of the three types of critical speech above, which do you struggle with the most? Why?

- Proverbs 6:16-18 says, *"There are six things that the LORD hates, seven that are an abomination to him..."* Look carefully at these seven sins and note how many relate to critical speech.

When James 4:12 says *"there is only one ... who is able to save and to destroy,"* this alludes to the fact that only God can determine someone's final spiritual destiny. The presence or absence of genuine faith in anyone falls to God alone to determine. We cannot conclude that when a brother or sister does or says something wrong, that means they are not really a Christian.

James' admonition not to judge others does not forbid us from asking a fellow Christ follower about their choices or even going to them to talk about a pattern of sin in their life. But according to the law of Christ, such confrontation is to be done out of love and concern for the one being confronted, not from a spirit of vengeance or mean criticism.

- Explain in your own words the difference between holding someone accountable for their words and actions and passing judgment on their eternal destiny.

- Can you think of an example from your life when you were either too passive or too aggressive in confronting others regarding their behavior? How can you live out your faith differently in the future?

A critical spirit can kill community in the Church. The Holy Spirit convicts us of sin and brings us to repentance, restoring community. Let's speak the truth in love and let God guide hearts.

JAMES 4:13-15

DAY 27
Boasting about tomorrow is not showing proper humility.

The number of planners and calendars available on Amazon.com could cause decision fatigue in the heartiest of online shoppers. In part, this abundance of options comes from something within us as humans that esteems time as indescribably sacred. We know we have a limited amount of it, and we want to make the most of it. We have heard warnings not to waste it from those who have lost it with the untimely passing of loved ones.

James' admonition regarding time focuses on the dangers of planning without a proper perspective. We cannot separate these exhortations in verses 13-15 from the previous verses in Chapter 4 dealing with chasing worldly pursuits and pleasures. James contrasts the futility of pursuing earthly gain with the brevity of life: *"For you are a mist that appears for a little time and then vanishes"* (v. 14c). In other words, he is saying, "Your life is so short! Why waste it on what is temporary?"

- Think through a typical day in your life. What takes up most of your time?

- In certain seasons of motherhood, we spend many hours of our days investing in our children. Or we may be investing in our grandchildren, working with excellence for our employers, or spending time elsewhere. List some examples of earthly investments you frequently make; then list eternal investments. What do you notice about your lists?

If we knew Jesus was returning for us tomorrow, what would we spend today doing? Or if we knew we only had one more day on earth, what would we most desire to accomplish? This is James' point. Would it be worthwhile to make more money? Own a particular item? Doubtful. Most of us would want to spend time with a person or do one last thing to make their lives better. We would not want to *"trade and make a profit"* (James 4:13) simply for profit's sake. We would see that the deeper purpose of worldly wealth is to bless others instead of only satisfying ourselves. James does not condemn making a profit in and of itself — rather, he questions the selfish motivation and the self-reliant attitude behind seeking wealth too eagerly.

James implores us to remember that the Lord holds the number of our days: *"If the Lord wills, we will live and do this or that"* (James 4:15). God gives us our time, and we are called to return it to Him by seeking His will for how to spend it. James has already repeatedly told us that part of how we spend our time should include taking care of people in need (James 1:27; James 2:15-16) and studying and obeying the Word of God (James 1:25). God gives us a limited number of days on earth; how can we use that time to please Him?

- How does the admonishment in James 4:14-15 echo Jesus' words in Matthew 6:19-21?

- In Psalm 90:12, what did Moses say will result in a proper perspective on time?

In Psalm 139:16, King David wrote that *"in [God's] book were written, every one of them, the days that were formed for me,"* reminding us God knew exactly when we would arrive on earth, and He knows exactly when we will depart. He has counted up our time here with purpose. Seeking His purpose for our lives keeps time in the proper perspective. Paul expounds upon this in Acts 17:26-27, saying God also determines exactly where we live, placing us in families, communities and workplaces according to *"allotted periods and the boundaries of [our] dwelling place[s]"* so that we *"should seek God."*

The days are long, but the years are short. Will we spend our time seeking God or something else?

- What is one practical way you can devote time this week to seeking God (in prayer, Bible reading, etc.) and serving others in His name?

JAMES 4:16-17

DAY 28
If we know the good we ought to do and do not do it, it is sin.

Imagine an employee who knows she has a review meeting with her boss approaching. From the beginning of her employment, her supervisor laid out specific job duties and expectations to best benefit the company. But instead, the employee came up with her own ideas about how she ought to spend her time, disregarding the boss's instructions. Certain her own strategy was better, she arrogantly spurned her boss's wisdom and authority.

The review meeting probably would not be celebratory.

In today's scriptures, James addressed wealthy Christians who made plans for their lives without acknowledging the ultimate boss: God. They did not seek God's will but leaned on self-reliance and personal strategy, seeking success. In their arrogance, they were certain of *their* ability to effectively carry out *their* plans (James 4:16).

- Have you ever been part of a team where someone repeatedly refused to follow directions and insisted on doing things their own way? How did that impact relationships and functionality?

- While some might label a person who marches to their own drum as "irresponsible," why do you think James used the word *"boasting"* in verse 16 to describe the act of disobeying God's directions for our lives?

- If we are not seeking God's will for our lives but are planning our courses of action without Him, why would that be *"evil"* (v. 16)? Is it evil even if we mean well?

Verse 17 seems hard to connect with the preceding idea of arrogance in planning without God. But a closer examination provides the link: We could easily focus on the things God says we are not supposed to do ... while still going about planning our own lives. We might think, *I don't murder, lie or steal — I just make decisions about how I spend my time without consulting God. That's not really a sin issue.* But God is after a heart attitude that seeks His direction for our time, our talents and everything else.

Interestingly, in Matthew 25, when Jesus talks about those condemned in the final judgment, He does not list the sins of *commission* — things people shouldn't have done but did. Instead He focuses on the sins of *omission* — things people should have done but didn't.

- According to Matthew 25:41-46, what do the condemned fail to do that causes Jesus' rebuke?

"Live with the end in mind." Have you ever heard that expression? It reminds us that life is short and that one day we will stand before Jesus and give an account of how we lived our lives. For believers, this accounting is not to determine whether or not we will spend eternity in heaven — Jesus already secured our place there through His death and resurrection. But Scripture makes it clear that Jesus will take stock of our works on earth and reward us accordingly (Luke 19:17; Matthew 6:1; Matthew 10:42; 1 Corinthians 3:13-14).

- How does Matthew 25:1-13, along with James 4:17, teach us to live with the end in mind?

Rather than asking God to reveal His overarching plan for our lives, James invites us to seek God's plan for the next moment, the next 15 minutes, and then the half-hour after that. We are to live in moment-by-moment dependence on God, who makes every moment count when we obediently submit to His guidance.

JAMES 5:1-3

DAY 29

James warned against hoarding wealth and exploiting others.

Buckle up and get ready, friends: James opens this chapter with some harsh warnings of judgment. Most scholars believe he was not speaking to fellow Christians here but to the wealthy non-Christian landowners of his day who exploited the poor. This may explain why he said *"come now, you rich"* in verse 1 but then *"be patient, therefore, brothers"* (referring to Christians) in verse 7.

At this time, land was predominantly owned by a small group of people who hired out day laborers to work their fields. These landowners grew increasingly rich while the majority of people lived on daily subsistence. James condemned the rich not for having wealth but for misusing it.[1]

The question becomes: Why would James write these warnings to people who would most likely never read his letter?

Scholars suggest a couple of reasons. First, we know some wealthy landowners were included in the congregation of believers James was addressing. He may have been making an indirect plea for them to be mindful of their ability to care for the poor and needy, as he had already admonished previously (James 1:27; James 2:15-17). Secondly, James 5:1-3 would have reminded his readers who were struggling to meet their daily needs, or who were treated unjustly by the rich, that God saw their plight. God will hold the rich accountable for their treatment of the poor.

- What is a situation in our day where you see injustice happening and it requires patience as you (or others) wait for God to act?

- Based upon James' letter thus far, how do you think he was asking his readers to respond to injustice in light of God's coming judgment? How might James' words of judgment against those who exploited wealth and power give hope to those who are suffering today?

James wrote here about the Day of Judgment when Jesus will return to bring justice to the earth. This could happen at any moment, so we are to live expectantly, showing love to our neighbors and sharing the message of Christ's salvation. Our primary focus is not on acquiring more and more wealth.

- How does Jesus describe the man who chases after riches in Luke 12:15-21?

Instead of wealth being utilized to bless others and bring life, James described *"corroded"* wealth in terms depicting death and decay. The statement that *"your gold ... will eat your flesh like fire"* (v. 3) is a symbol of God's judgment against those who use their riches for sinful purposes. In Ezekiel 16:49, God pronounced similar judgment on the people of a city called Sodom, saying they were prideful, overindulgent, and lacking in concern for the poor. God saw their behavior and *"removed them"* from the earth (Ezekiel 16:50).

- What warning did Jesus give concerning wealth in Matthew 19:23-25? Why do you think this was so astonishing to His audience?

Wealth can lead to self-reliance. When we think we can buy everything we need, we're tempted to think we can stop depending upon God. But James reminds us to look around and see how our blessings can be used to bless others!

- Who can you bless today with your time, talents, money, attention or other resources?

JAMES 5:4-6

DAY 30
James assured that rich oppressors will face judgment.

"Give us this day our daily bread ..." (Matthew 6:11). Jesus taught His disciples to make this request of God in the Lord's Prayer. In modern Western culture, we could see this as an admonition not to desire excess, but to Jesus' original audience, daily bread was most likely their reality. The average person during the time of Jesus lived day to day, with just enough to get by.

In today's scriptures from James, once again, he was likely not addressing fellow Christians but wealthy people who denied Christ and deprived the poor (James 5:4). In Leviticus 19:13, God commanded, *"You shall not oppress your neighbor or rob him. The wages of a hired worker shall not remain with you all night until the morning."* To refuse to pay a laborer at the end of the day meant he and his family might go hungry all night. What James specifically meant by saying *"you kept back [wages] by fraud"* (James 5:4) could include a refusal to pay at the end of the day or a change in payment from the agreed-upon price.

- What could be some modern-day equivalents to this kind of oppression or day-by-day living in our culture? How can the Church care for people in these situations?

In the Jewish world, to deprive a person of daily support was essentially the same as murdering them (v. 6). The hoarders of wealth had the ability to help but chose not to, so the lavish lifestyle of the landowners stood as a witness against them when viewed in contrast to the steep poverty of the exploited workers. But the cries of the poor did not go unnoticed by God.

The *"Lord of hosts,"* as James referenced in verse 4, is a name for God depicting Him as the general of a heavenly army. Here we see that the cries of the oppressed rouse Him to go to battle to fight on their behalf.

- What comfort do you find in God as the Lord of hosts? In what area of your life do you need God to go to battle for you today?

To the exploited, James 5:4-6 was a promise of deliverance. To the landowner, it was a warning of punishment. Farmers would usually fatten their livestock right before slaughter, but James used irony in verse 5 to show how the hearts of these wealthy landowners were fattened by the luxuries of life, only to be doomed on the day of God's judgment. The day laborers living for their next meal had not rebelled against or resisted those exploiting them (v. 6), but God would bring justice. He will only allow His people to be unjustly oppressed for so long until He goes to battle against their oppressors.

- Why do you think many people do not fear God's judgment? How might being aware of this judgment spur us on to share and live out our faith?

- How do you determine the difference between what God has invited us to enjoy in life versus self-indulgence (v. 5)? What are some practical ways we can guard against materialism?

God will judge those who live for themselves and refuse to follow Him. While James didn't know how many would hear his letter, let alone respond in repentance, he did not fail to warn them. Will we follow his example by warning others in our time that God will punish the unjust? Praise God that we can also tell others about His mercy, which is available to remove us from His wrath if we trust in Jesus for salvation!

How would living in a continual awareness of Jesus' imminent return change the way you spend your money or your time? What changes might the Lord be prompting you to make in your life in response to today's reading?

WEEK SIX

Reflection & Prayer:

In Luke 11:34, Jesus says: *"Your eye is the lamp of your body. When your eye is healthy, your whole body is full of light, but when it is bad, your body is full of darkness."* Some scholars suggest that when He said this, Jesus was quoting a contemporary rabbi of His day, Rabbi Eliezer, who taught the following:

"The key to following a good path in life is to have a 'good eye'—an open and generous nature. Judging others charitably. Being a good friend and a good neighbor. To receive every person with joy. The one who has a good eye has a good heart. The person with a bad eye has a possessive or envious heart. A person with a bad eye will be driven out of this world."[1]

In this week's readings, James implored us to have a good eye toward our fellow people (especially fellow Christians); to be mindful of the brevity of life; and to remain focused on God as we spend our time, treasures and talents.

Are we charitable in our judgment of others? When we see others making or being hurt by destructive choices, do we humbly remind ourselves, *But for the grace of God, there go I?* Are we generous to those in need, or are we possessive and envious? Let's reflect on these questions this weekend as we live out our faith through the wisdom found in James.

Dear Jesus, how easy it is to think our righteousness depends solely on the bad things we don't do: murder, cheat, steal or lie ... But we forget the good things we ought to do: encourage, speak life, care for others and esteem them. How we treat other people and how readily we notice their needs speaks of the condition of our hearts. Help us to love our neighbors as ourselves. Help us to speak to others and about others with generosity and kindness. Help us to see others with a good eye, Lord. Forgive us when we become critical or judgmental, withholding love and mercy that we ourselves do not deserve but that You give us so generously. Help us to be giving in return. In Jesus' name, amen.

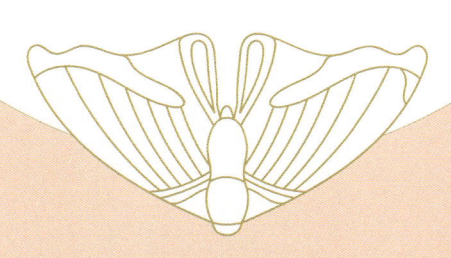

NOTES

NOTES

week seven

AM I DOING THIS RIGHT? HOW TO LIVE OUT YOUR *Faith* THROUGH THE *Wisdom* FOUND IN JAMES

FAITH

wisdom

AM I DOING THIS RIGHT?
BOOK of JAMES — *Faith Through Wisdom*

JAMES 5:7-9

DAY 31

James taught that Christians can be patient like a farmer waiting for rain.

The 19th-century author E.M. Bounds once said, "I think Christians fail so often to get answers to their prayers because they do not wait long enough on God."[1] But oh how difficult it can be to wait! While we work, our patience mildly persists, but when there is nothing left to do but wait, impatience madly erupts.

In his teaching on waiting in James 5:7-9, James used a farming illustration for his agrarian audience, many of whom worked fields or lived near them. Once the farmer prepared the soil, planted the crops, and guarded them from weeds and pestilence, he practiced patience. He waited on God to send rain for the crops to grow (v. 7). He guarded the work he had done, but without God's provision, his work would be in vain. For all the years of their lives, James' readers had witnessed God's faithfulness season after season to bring to fruition the work of their hands. As a people desperate for God to come through for them, they would be reminded in whom their hope remained. Jesus was and is coming (v. 8).

Imagine the farmer waiting and watching his fields through scarce early rains. Would the later rains be plentiful enough to save his crops? Sometimes our perception of scarcity in God's activity to alleviate our difficulty causes anxiety. When things do not go our way, our human nature searches for someone to blame. We begin to grumble and complain and view others critically. But instead of groaning and grumbling, James says we are to *"establish [our] hearts"* (v. 8).

- How are our hearts established or strengthened according to Romans 16:25 and 2 Thessalonians 3:3? What other implications can we draw from this truth?

- What is a prayer you currently have that requires great patience? Do you feel as though there is a scarcity of activity on God's part? How does James' reminder of God's faithfulness encourage you to remain patient?

Faith requires practice to continue to guard the seeds we have sown. Much as a farmer surveys his land and removes threats and thieves, all while waiting on God, so we do the same spiritually. James' admonition to *"be patient"* (James 5:7-8) did not involve a passive resignation toward the injustices of his day.[2] Rather, James prompted his readers to recognize that while some circumstances were beyond their control, a reckoning would occur, as everyone remains accountable to Christ.

The time of harvest is often used to describe a time of judgment in Scripture. Jesus, the rightful Judge, will return and hold all people to account, including those who have rebelled against Him, exploited others and committed evil. In Matthew 13:39b, explaining one of His parables, Jesus said, *"The harvest is the end of the age, and the reapers are angels."*

- Do you view prayer as a first response or a last resort in difficulty as you wait on Jesus' return/harvest? How might going to God in prayer over difficult situations reduce grumbling (James 5:9)?

- Read through Psalm 37:5-14. Which verses bring you the greatest comfort in your own area of waiting on God?

Jesus will ask us, His people, how we waited for the day of His return. Did we endure difficulty and bear with one another patiently? Let's close with the words of 2 Thessalonians 2:16-17: *"Now may our Lord Jesus Christ himself, and God our Father, who loved us and gave us eternal comfort and good hope through grace, comfort [our] hearts and establish [us] in every good work and word."*

JAMES 5:10-12

DAY 32
James encouraged Christians to consider the prophets and Job as examples to have integrity in our speech.

In the Old Testament, the Lord raised up prophets to deliver messages to His people. They spoke of God's power, holiness, faithfulness and compassion. Their speech also included warnings of future judgment and calls to repentance. But the people of God often didn't respond obediently to these messages; Jesus said the people hated, reviled, spoke against and even murdered the prophets (Luke 6:22-23; Luke 11:47-48). Despite knowing that their words would invoke the people's wrath or even incite violence, the prophets faithfully spoke messages from the Lord — which is why James tells us to consider and imitate the prophets *"as an example of suffering and patience"* (James 5:10).

- What happened to the prophet Jeremiah when he spoke the words of God to the people of Jerusalem in Jeremiah 38:1-6?

- According to Ezekiel 2:1-10, what kind of words did he have to deliver to the people? How is Ezekiel's long-suffering as a prophet described in verse 6?

- Describe the prophet Elijah's mental and emotional state after obeying the Lord in 1 Kings 19:1-4.

These prophets spoke out against the sinfulness of how people lived in comparison to the holiness of God, so they did not find much popularity among the people of their day. But today we applaud their obedience to God in spite of such difficulty: *"We consider those blessed who remained steadfast"* (James 5:11a).

Although Job was not a prophet, James also mentions him in verse 11. Some scholars suggest a Jewish work entitled *The Testament of Job* was written around the time of James and caused him to cite Job here. This book credits Job as saying, "Patience is better than anything."[1]

- Read about what happened to Job in Job 1:13-22 and how he responded. Then read Job 42:12-17. How does Job's life also remind us of God's compassion and mercy toward those who are patiently faithful to Him?

James' point was not to promise his readers their own restoration of material wealth before eternity, as Job received. Instead James pointed to the final purpose of God: to display His mercy and love and reveal the full blessing that awaits believers in the new heaven and new earth (Revelation 21).

- What does 1 Peter 5:10 promise that God will do for us after our suffering on earth?

Our current stage of life is not the end of our story. We will see the mercy of God and experience His compassion for all eternity. Knowing this, like Job, we can determine to maintain our integrity in the midst of suffering (Job 27:4-6; Job 31).

When others persecute or mistreat us, how tempting it could be to say what we think might ease our suffering — but James sees integrity in speech as proof *"above all"* of the integrity of our hearts and lives (James 5:12). James previously taught that the one who controls their tongue is *"able also to bridle his whole body"* (James 3:2). Rather than trying to invoke certain words (an *"oath"*) to gain trust, James commands us to live in such a way that our trustworthiness is already evident (James 5:12).

- Read Matthew 5:34-37, and note the similarities to James 5:12. How might swearing to follow through on our words *"[come] from evil"* (Matthew 5:37)?

We are called to live lives of integrity, not look for loopholes to justify renegotiating our promises. Life undoubtedly holds unexpected and extenuating circumstances where we will find ourselves unable to follow through. Those things we cannot control. But an unwavering attitude of obedience to God, even when the sacrifice feels heavy, invites God's compassion and mercy toward us.

JAMES 5:13-15

DAY 33
James urged believers to pray for those who were in trouble, were sick or had sinned.

In the fictional book *The Screwtape Letters,* C.S. Lewis writes from the perspective of a character called Wormwood, a demon working against Christians. Lewis imagines this demon saying, "The best thing, where it is possible, is to keep the [Christian] from the serious intention of praying altogether."[1]

We often think of our enemy tempting us to sin, but he also tries to keep us from praying — and he trembles when he cannot stop us. As James began to wrap up his letter full of quips, commands and difficult calls to action, he implored his readers to employ the power of prayer. For Jews, prayer had always been commanded (in the Old Testament) as a regular part of their lives. But here James reminded Christians to remember prayer's power rather than simply treat it as a routine or ritual.

- List two or three of the biggest distractions in your life that keep you from praying. What are some practical ways you can minimize these distractions?

James emphasized the need to pray in all kinds of circumstances: suffering, cheerfulness and sickness (James 5:13-14). In adversity, he encouraged prayerfully turning to God for comfort and healing. In blessing, he encouraged praise. How easy it can be to forget God when our daily needs are met and our lives seem secure! Yet the command to pray is written in the present tense for all of these varied circumstances, implying an ongoing, continual habit of prayer in any situation.

- Do you tend to pray more often when things are difficult or when things are going well? Why do you think this is so?

A few aspects of verses 13-14 can create confusion or controversy, so let's dig into the ideas here:

First, how to define the *"elders of the church"* (v. 14). In the first-century Jewish world, "elder" referred loosely to those in authority as well as those who had lived for many years and gained knowledge through experience. The early Church did not delineate between pastors and elders as some Christian denominations do today, and most likely James referred to both roles in verse 14.[2]

Second, we see these church leaders were to *"pray over [the sick], anointing him with oil in the name of the Lord"* (v. 14). Though the oil itself held no healing power, all healing comes from God. The oil served as a symbol of consecration, a tangible sign reminding all who were present that the anointed person was set apart for God's care and attention to their need. They belonged to God, and He heard their prayers.

James' writing also implies that those who were sick had limited mobility or perhaps were bedridden since the elders were called to go to them (v. 14) in contrast to the sick being brought to the elders or coming before them of their own volition. In the ancient world, without modern medicine and mobility aids, sickness or injury often resulted in isolation.

- How might isolation make illness even more difficult to bear? How can the community of the Church aid those who are suffering in this way?

- Do you ever feel forgotten by God? How might other believers praying for you help you feel known and loved?

Finally, James says, *"the prayer of faith will save the one who is sick."* James also says *"he will be forgiven"* and adds an important condition: *"if he has committed sins"* (v. 15). This reminds us that illness is not always — perhaps not even usually — caused by a person's own choices. All sickness is caused by the presence of sin and death in our fallen world, but this does not mean all sickness is a punishment for individual sins, nor does it mean that repenting of sin guarantees physical healing.

The hard part to reconcile is when we pray for healing and nothing happens. Was it not a *"prayer of faith"* (v. 15)? Sometimes we second-guess or shame ourselves for what feels like a failed prayer — but that's when we can remember that the power of prayer doesn't come from us. It comes from God. And He never fails, though He sometimes answers our prayers differently than we desire. We are to pray *"in the name of the Lord"* (v. 14), believing that if it be God's will, healing will certainly be granted. But to pray in the name of the Lord also means we submit to His will for the circumstance we are bringing before Him. Jesus Himself prayed, *"Let this cup pass from me; nevertheless, not as I will, but as you will"* (Matthew 26:39).

- Have you ever felt ashamed for not having enough faith in prayer? How does today's passage remind you that God's yeses and noes to our requests reflect a greater understanding that we cannot always comprehend?

Prayer unites us to God and to each other. *"Bear[ing] one another's burdens,"* as Scripture says in Galatians 6:2, involves bringing them before God's throne and asking Him to bring comfort.

JAMES 5:16-18

DAY 34
The prayers of the righteous are powerful.

Whenever we come across the word "therefore" in Scripture, we can always ask ourselves, *What is it there for?* In other words, what is the "how" and "why" behind this conclusion or command?

James tells us, *"Therefore, confess your sins to one another and pray for one another, that you may be healed"* (James 5:16a). Why? Because if someone is sick, their body can be healed through prayer. If someone has sinned, their soul can be healed as their sins are forgiven through confession and prayer. The Apostle John tells us similarly that *"if we confess our sins, [God] is faithful and just to forgive us our sins and to cleanse us from all unrighteousness"* (1 John 1:9).

Notably, James commands *all* believers to pray in verse 16a, not just church elders. Yet a strong clue as to why many believers may struggle with prayer is found in verse 16b: *"The prayer of a righteous person has great power as it is working."* Our enemy works hard to keep us from praying, and one tactic he often uses is to hurl our unrighteous acts and attitudes toward us in condemnation. He hisses accusations, insisting that our prayers are not worthy to be uttered in light of our own sinfulness or that they have no effect. And he shames us into silence.

- It's true that we're imperfect, sinful people. But according to Romans 5:17, where does our righteousness come from if we are in Christ? How does this give us power to pray?

- Do you ever feel unworthy to bring your desires or emotions before God in prayer? How does James' teaching remind us that God longs for us to bring our hurts, heartaches, requests and sins before Him?

We may hesitate to compare our faith to that of a mighty prophet like Elijah, who is mentioned in James 5:17-18. Elijah served as a prophet during the reign of Ahab and Jezebel in the northern kingdom of Israel. This wicked duo killed most of the prophets and priests of God and established the worship of the false god Baal throughout Israel. All alone, Elijah marched up to the palace and confronted Ahab, declaring God's judgment upon the land (the drought referenced in James 5:17). Later, Elijah staged a showdown against the prophets of Baal to prove who was the true God: Yahweh or Baal. After God brought fire from heaven to consume Elijah's sacrifice while Baal remained mute and distant, the people of Israel fell on their faces in repentance, and God sent rain across the land (1 Kings 17-18).

Elijah doesn't sound like the average guy in your neighborhood, does he? So what is James getting at? This miraculous rainmaker had passions and emotions just like us. He struggled with doubt, discouragement and disobedience just like us. But one thing Elijah did do — he resolved to pray. And through his prayers, God did mighty things.

We do not need to be mighty to pray. We just need to believe in our mighty God.

- In what ways does Elijah's story inspire you to pray fervently and ask God to move in the hearts of people and their situations?

Elijah's story also teaches us that faith does not eliminate all hardship from our lives. Elijah lived in isolation, traveled far away from home to hide from persecutors until it was time to return to Israel, and took great risks to obey God. For James' original readers, many of whom were removed from Israel themselves due to persecution, Elijah's story would have held special meaning. At the end of Elijah's life, God also answered his prayers by sending him Elisha to be a co-laborer in God's Kingdom plans (1 Kings 19:15-21).

- Has God asked something difficult of you lately? How does Elijah's story encourage you?

- Have you ever asked God to send you a co-laborer in His Kingdom plans for you? How might having a prayer partner help you live out your faith as God has called you to do?

God longs to bring fruitfulness through our lives as we seek Him in prayer. Rather than only asking God to remove suffering, we can also ask Him to produce fruit in others' lives as He brings healing of all kinds: physical, mental, emotional and spiritual (James 5:16).

4 T'S:
A Framework for Partnering in Prayer

When we're walking through something difficult, it's a great comfort to have a friend beside us. As we all go through *"trials of various kinds"* and tests in our lives (James 1:2), the four T's below can provide a simple framework for an accountability or prayer partner. Discussing these four T's regularly with a trusted fellow believer — face to face or even through text messaging, phone call or video chat — can provide a way to gain strength from and offer strength to one another.

1. TRIAL.

This is something you are facing over which you have very little control. It is a call to faith and prayer. Some examples could be a health diagnosis, a job loss, being cut out of a relationship, etc. These are hard things in life that leave us feeling overwhelmed. Sharing them with a friend and asking for prayer helps lighten the load.

2. TEST.

This is something you are facing that may be difficult but that gives you a choice to be obedient and follow biblical Truth in response to the circumstance. This is a call to obedience. For instance: a chance to respond to a difficult co-worker, exhibit patience toward a family member, trust God with your finances, etc. These are situations that you face in which you must make a decision. Will you turn to God and seek His direction or rely on worldly wisdom? Ask your prayer partner to pray for God to give you His wisdom in your situation.

3. TESTIMONY.

This is something you've seen God do in your life — a prayer answered, an unexpected blessing, a victory in obedience — or even a story you heard from someone else. Sharing how God is working boosts your faith as you intentionally pause to reflect on His activity in your life. And it also blesses your prayer partner when they see God responding to their prayers over you.

4. TRUTH.

This is a Bible verse or passage you might send to your prayer/accountability partner to encourage them in whatever they are going through. Sharing God's Truth helps us keep our eyes from becoming too laser-focused on our own problems and helps us develop the habit of going to the Word of God in hard times. We can seek answers to life's questions and trials in Scripture, trusting God to speak to us through His Word.

HERE'S A SAMPLE OF A FOUR T'S TEXT YOU COULD SEND TO YOUR PRAYER/ACCOUNTABILITY PARTNER:

Hi, friend! Here are my four T's this week!

TRIAL
Prayer for God to provide financially for our car to be repaired.

TEST
I want to show kindness to my neighbor after she yelled at me about keeping my trash cans out. Pray for an opportunity to bless her.

TESTIMONY
Praising God that my son passed his English test this week!

TRUTH
Psalm 46:10a says, *"Be still, and know that I am God."* As you are waiting on answers for your health diagnosis, friend, I just want to remind you God is in control and He loves you!

Who could you approach to become a four T's partner or accountability group? We are always better together!

JAMES 5:19-20

DAY 35
Bringing a wandering believer back to faith is a noble act.

Dietrich Bonhoeffer, a German pastor and theologian who was martyred for his stance against Nazi Germany, spent his life establishing training schools for pastors. In his book *Life Together,* he wrote, "Nothing can be more cruel than the leniency which abandons others to their sin. Nothing can be more compassionate than the severe reprimand which calls another Christian in one's community back from the path of sin."[1]

James would heartily shout, "Amen!" When one in our Christian community begins to wander, James implores us to lovingly bring them back.

- Why would it be cruel to withhold loving correction from someone who is trying to justify sin in their life?

- How does our culture twist this idea and claim that leniency toward sin is actually kindness?

It is interesting that James concludes his letter with this command to bring back wanderers in James 5:19 — and that it follows his command to pray in James 5:16. If prayer alone is not enough to turn the wandering saint around, more direct action is to be taken. Here James is not referring to evangelism, or inviting unbelievers to repent and begin to follow Christ. He says *"anyone among you"* (v. 19), with *"you"* being the Church, referring to someone who at least outwardly has identified themselves as following Christ. When we see a fellow believer straying away from Christ's commands, we need to go get them.

- What warnings did Paul issue in Galatians 6:1-5 regarding restoring a wandering Christian? Why is it important not to *"think [we are] something"* as Christ followers?

- Have you ever had a fellow believer confront you about a sin in your life? How did you receive their words?

Scholars think the mention of wandering in James 5:19-20 relates to the imagery of God's people as sheep — creatures who are prone to stray from the flock and constantly need redirecting — throughout Scripture. Specifically, James may have been alluding to Ezekiel 34, where God issued harsh judgment against Israel's shepherds' lack of concern for their sheep (metaphorically, the leaders' lack of care for the people). In Ezekiel 34:4, God said, *"The weak you have not strengthened, the sick you have not healed, the injured you have not bound up, the strayed you have not brought back, the lost you have not sought, and with force and harshness you have ruled them."*

In contrast, Jesus says, *"I am the good shepherd. The good shepherd lays down his life for the sheep"* (John 10:11). In so doing, Jesus fulfills God's promise in Ezekiel 34:12: *"As a shepherd seeks out his flock when he is among his sheep that have been scattered, so will I seek out my sheep, and I will rescue them from all places where they have been scattered on a day of clouds and thick darkness."*

James implores us to follow Christ's example to seek out those who have strayed; in doing so, we *"will save [their] soul from death and will cover a multitude of sins"* (James 5:20). This doesn't mean we ourselves can actually redeem anyone — only Jesus can do that. But if we pursue a wandering brother or sister and they return to Christ, they will be spared from spiritual death and prevented from committing many sins while in a state of rebellion.

- In what ways are you intentionally involved in Christian community? What steps can you take to make this a regular part of living out your faith?

James closes his letter by holding up two pillars for gaining wisdom and following Christ: prayer and Christian community. Both require intentionality, grace and grit to keep pursuing. But James promises this is the path to becoming *"perfect and complete, lacking in nothing"* (James 1:4). It may not be easy, but Jesus' way is the right way!

WEEK SEVEN

Reflection & Prayer:

Patience and prayer: possibly two of the hardest parts of how to live out our faith in Christ day by day. Prayer affirms our trust that God will indeed hear us and respond according to His will, and prayer also makes us more patient in the waiting. It reminds us that God is in control of all circumstances, ruling the world in His infinite wisdom and ever mindful of us in our circumstances.

Sometimes we may surrender ourselves to the belief that when we don't know what to do, "all we can do" is pray as a last resort. But according to James, prayer is often the *most effective* thing we can do! At times when circumstances are so far beyond our ability to control, James reminds us prayer *"has great power"* (James 5:16).

We may not always understand exactly how prayer works, but we can experience its power. Testimonies of God's mighty answers to prayer abound in the lives of His saints. We also know of stories where God did not answer prayers in the way we had hoped, yet He entered into our disappointment to help us patiently seek to understand His ways in light of eternity. Even when we cannot reconcile His actions with our situations, we can trust that we ourselves are reconciled to Him forever through faith in Christ.

We may not always know the right answer, but we always know the right One to call. Our God will be faithful to answer our prayers.

Psalm 34:17-19 brings great hope as we call out to God: *"When the righteous cry for help, the Lord hears and delivers them out of all their troubles. The Lord is near to the brokenhearted and saves the crushed in spirit. Many are the afflictions of the righteous, but the Lord delivers him out of them all."*

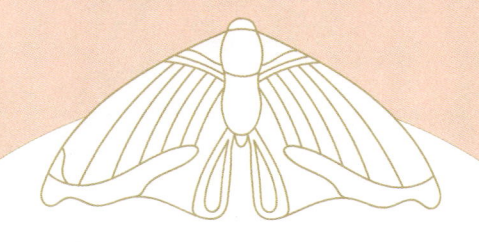

Dear Jesus, may we first turn to You when we don't know what to do, remembering that You long to give us wisdom and power to respond to Your will for our lives. Thank You that You always hear us when we pray and that Your heart is moved with compassion toward us. You surround us in our circumstances, offering Your peace, strength and help. In Jesus' name, amen.

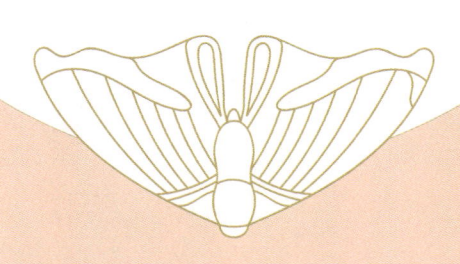

NOTES

NOTES

ENDNOTES

Welcome to James
1. Walvoord, John F. and Roy B. Zuck. *The Bible Knowledge Commentary: New Testament.* Colorado Springs, CO: David C. Cook, 1983, p. 819.

Who Was James? A Lost Brother Found
1. Keener, Craig S. *The IVP Bible Background Commentary: New Testament.* Downers Grove, IL: IVP Academic, 2014, p. 669.

What Issues Did James and the Early Church Face?
1. Keener, Craig S. *The IVP Bible Background Commentary: New Testament.* Downers Grove, IL: IVP Academic, 2014, p. 669.
2. Keener, Craig S. *The IVP Bible Background Commentary: New Testament.* Downers Grove, IL: IVP Academic, 2014, p. 312.
3. Hart, John F. *James: The Moody Bible Commentary.* Edited by Michael Rydelnik and Michael Vanlaningham, Chicago, IL: Moody Publishers, 2014, p. 1947.

James' Truth for Today: The Wisdom We Need Is in the Word
1. Moo, Douglas J. *The Letter of James: The Pillar New Testament Commentary.* Edited by D.A. Carson, Grand Rapids, MI: William B. Eerdmans Publishing Company, 2021, p. 8.

Day 2
1. Hart, John F. *James: The Moody Bible Commentary.* Edited by Michael Rydelnik and Michael Vanlaningham, Chicago, IL: Moody Publishers, 2014, p. 1947.

Day 3
1. Moo, Douglas J. *The Letter of James: The Pillar New Testament Commentary.* Edited by D.A. Carson, Grand Rapids, MI: William B. Eerdmans Publishing Company, 2021, p. 86.
2. Moo, Douglas J. *The Letter of James: The Pillar New Testament Commentary.* Edited by D.A. Carson, Grand Rapids, MI: William B. Eerdmans Publishing Company, 2021, pp. 84-85.

Day 5
1. Kittel, Gerhard, Geoffrey W. Bromiley, and Gerhard Friedrich, eds. *Theological Dictionary of the New Testament.* Grand Rapids, MI: William B. Eerdmans Publishing Company, 1964.

Biblical Word Study: Shalom
1. Lookadoo, Jonathon. "Peace," *Lexham Theological Wordbook.* Edited by Douglas Mangum, Derek R. Brown, Rachel Klippenstein, and Rebekah Hurst, Bellingham, WA: Lexham Press, 2014.
2. Elwell, Walter A. and Barry J. Beitzel. "Peace," *Baker Encyclopedia of the Bible.* Grand Rapids, MI: Baker Book House, 1988.

Day 16
1. Moo, Douglas J. *The Letter of James: The Pillar New Testament Commentary.* Edited by D.A. Carson, Grand Rapids, MI: William B. Eerdmans Publishing Company, 2021, p. 180.

Day 20
1. Platt, David. *Christ-Centered Exposition: Exalting Jesus in James.* Nashville, TN: Holman Reference, 2014.

Day 23
1. Keener, Craig S. *The IVP Bible Background Commentary: New Testament.* Downers Grove, IL: IVP Academic, 2014, p. 677.
2. Mangum, Douglas, Derek R. Brown, Rachel Klippenstein, and Rebekah Hurst, eds. *Lexham Theological Wordbook.* Bellingham, WA: Lexham Press, 2014.
3. Newton, John. "Dependence on Christ—God's Prescriptions," 1775, The Reformed Reader, https://www.reformedreader.org/rbb/newton/letter04.htm.

Week Five Reflection & Prayer
1. Chesterton, G.K. "If I Had Only One Sermon To Preach," *The Common Man.* 1930.

Day 26
1. *"Katalaleó." Strong's Concordance,* Bible Hub, https://biblehub.com/greek/2635.htm.
2. Moo, Douglas J. *The Letter of James: The Pillar New Testament Commentary.* Edited by D.A. Carson, Grand Rapids, MI: William B. Eerdmans Publishing Company, 2021, p. 249.

Day 29
1. Moo, Douglas J. *The Letter of James: The Pillar New Testament Commentary.* Edited by D.A. Carson, Grand Rapids, MI: William B. Eerdmans Publishing Company, 2021, p. 267.

Week Six Reflection & Prayer
1. Berkson, William and Menachem Fisch. *Pirke Avot: Timeless Wisdom for Modern Life.* Philadelphia, PA: The Jewish Publication Society, 2010.

Day 31
1. Bounds, E.M. "A Praying Pulpit Begets a Praying Pew," *The Complete Works of E. M. Bounds.* Start Publishing, 2012.
2. Moo, Douglas J. *The Letter of James: The Pillar New Testament Commentary.* Edited by D.A. Carson, Grand Rapids, MI: William B. Eerdmans Publishing Company, 2021, p. 281.

Day 32
1. Moo, Douglas J. *The Letter of James: The Pillar New Testament Commentary.* Edited by D.A. Carson, Grand Rapids, MI: William B. Eerdmans Publishing Company, 2021, p. 290.

Day 33
1. Lewis, C.S. *The Screwtape Letters,* San Francisco, CA: HarperCollins, 2001, pp. 15-19.
2. Moo, Douglas J. *The Letter of James: The Pillar New Testament Commentary.* Edited by D.A. Carson, Grand Rapids, MI: William B. Eerdmans Publishing Company, 2021, p. 303.

Day 35
1. Bonhoeffer, Dietrich. *Life Together: Dietrich Bonhoeffer Works—Reader's Edition.* Edited by Victoria J. Barnett and Geffrey B. Kelly, Fortress Press, 2015, p. 107.

IF YOU LOVED JAMES,
WE THINK YOU'LL LOVE
OUR NEXT STUDY...

Proverbs:
Everyday Guidance for Making Everyday Decisions

AVAILABLE MAY 2024
AT P31BOOKSTORE.COM.